What Kind of Parent Am I?

What Kind of Parent Am I?

Self-Surveys That Reveal the
Impact of Toxic Stress and More

Dr. Nicole Letourneau

DUNDURN
TORONTO

Printer: Webcom
Cover design: Laura Boyle
Cover images: From left to right, top to bottom: Istock.com/kokouu; shutterstock.com/wavebreakmedia; shutterstock.com/asph; Istock.com/UberImages; istock.com/Choreograph; shutterstock.com/Purino

Library and Archives Canada Cataloguing in Publication
Letourneau, Nicole, author
        What kind of parent am I? : self-surveys that reveal the impact of
toxic stress and more / Nicole Letourneau.

(Scientific parenting)
Includes bibliographical references.
Issued in print and electronic formats.
ISBN 978-1-4597-3900-0 (softcover).--ISBN 978-1-4597-3901-7 (PDF).--
ISBN 978-1-4597-3902-4 (EPUB)

        1. Parenting. 2. Child rearing. 3. Child development. 4. Parental
influences. I. Title.

HQ769.L478 2018   306.874   C2018-901689-2
                                                       C2018-901690-6

1   2   3   4   5   22   21   20   19   18

  Canada

We acknowledge the support of the **Canada Council for the Arts**, which last year invested $153 million to bring the arts to Canadians throughout the country, and the **Ontario Arts Council** for our publishing program. We also acknowledge the financial support of the **Government of Ontario**, through the **Ontario Book Publishing Tax Credit** and the **Ontario Media Development Corporation**, and the **Government of Canada**.

Nous remercions le **Conseil des arts du Canada** de son soutien. L'an dernier, le Conseil a investi 153 millions de dollars pour mettre de l'art dans la vie des Canadiennes et des Canadiens de tout le pays.

Care has been taken to trace the ownership of copyright material used in this book. The author and the publisher welcome any information enabling them to rectify any references or credits in subsequent editions.
                                                                    — J. Kirk Howard, President

The publisher is not responsible for websites or their content unless they are owned by the publisher.

Printed and bound in Canada.

VISIT US AT

dundurn.com | @dundurnpress | dundurnpress | dundurnpress

Dundurn
3 Church Street, Suite 500
Toronto, Ontario, Canada
M5E 1M2

For my husband, Dean Mullin,
and sons, Maxwell and Jackson

Contents

Preface

Almost as soon as I completed my first book, *Scientific Parenting: What Science Reveals About Parental Influence*, people started asking me when my next book would be coming out. I vividly remember one such conversation. I was excited to be interviewed about the book by Tralee Pearce of the *Globe and Mail*. I was thrilled to be talking about the successful culmination of a couple years' hard work, only to realize (with a bit of dismay) that there had to be a part two. In my discussion with Tralee, she pointed out that *Scientific Parenting* was a book on *why* parenting was important and that what I needed to do next was write a book on *how* best to parent. I was inspired by Tralee's question, if not a little overwhelmed at the apparent task ahead.

When I considered the follow-up book, I realized that I did not want to write yet another self-help book or argue that parents should adopt a certain style of parenting. So many books, magazines, and journal articles describe the various types of parenting, covering helicopter parenting, free-range parenting, tiger parenting, authoritative parenting, and attachment parenting, to name a few. The latest type, resilience parenting, is the new favourite of millennial parents who seek to encourage in their children effective coping with day-to-day life stressors in order to better prepare them for the world outside of the family fold.

While these parenting types garner a lot of media attention, you may be surprised to learn they are not generally taken seriously by social scientists who focus their careers on studying how parents affect their children's development. The truth is, there is very little scientific study on how these types of parenting affect children. With the exception of Baumrind's four types of parenting — authoritarian, authoritative, permissive, or neglectful — there is little to no scientific basis to support any of these approaches and how they may affect child development. It is well established that Baumrind's authoritative style, characterized by clear limit setting and child monitoring, does link to more optimal child development over time. However, how an authoritative style happens in the earliest relationships with newborn babies (for example, limit setting) or how other contextual factors like everyday or chronic stress affect parents' ability to be authoritative is not well understood. In my estimation, parenting styles are pop-culture characterizations at worst and philosophies of parenting at best, and are not scientifically validated.

What I wanted to do was write a book that objectively answered my long-standing question: What kind of parent am I? I wanted answers to questions such as How does my personal and family history affect how I parent? How do my current social circumstances affect how I parent? Is toxic stress affecting my parenting? What kind of support do I need? and Where can I get help to parent most effectively? After reading parenting advice books and studying parenting from every angle for over twenty years, knowing what kind of parent I am is something I should know a lot about. Yet before writing this book, I was still unsure. None of the parenting books I had read over the years had answered that question to my satisfaction — they never seemed to apply to me and *my* parenting situation.

So what was the best way forward? I could ask my children what kind of parent they think I am. When they were younger, like so many young children, they likely would have hugged my legs and said that I was the "best mom in the world." While melting my heart, this is not exactly an unbiased opinion. But at their ages now (teenager and young adult), I am sure they would first look at me like I am insane, then offer their standard sarcastic answers. While entertaining, this would not help answer my question. Alternatively, I could just keep doing my best and wait to see how they turn out. After all, if they grow up to be independent, get jobs, and attain and maintain healthy intimate relationships (dating partners, spouses) then I will feel that I have been successful. But I might always wonder if they would have done as well, in spite of me. Did what I do make a difference? It would be nice to know that I am on the right track, from more than just my observations of them.

I could ask my husband and he would likely be reassuring. I know we both try hard to be good parents and support and forgive each other in circumstances that are not always ideal. Family members, friends, colleagues, and others could be asked to venture their opinion, but again, it would be weird to ask. None of these options have ever felt very satisfying.

But being a good parent is important to me and I have always thought how gratifying it would be to know, from an objective, credible source, how I am likely doing. I also thought it would be good to know if there are any risks to my parenting that I should know about. I wanted to know if there are legacies from my history that could affect my parenting and my children's development. I wanted to know my strengths too — then I could address those risky legacies and be comforted by my strengths as a parent.

I have often thought how helpful it would be to be assessed, like so many of my research participants have been, to know what kind of parent I am. We ask parents in our studies questions about their family history, mental health history, stress, relationships, attitudes toward parenting, and the like. We then use that data to make predictions about how their children will do. And, importantly, these factors *do* predict how well children develop and grow over time.

Why not use similar research assessments in my follow-up book, I thought, to give parents a profile of how they are doing and a sense of their risks and strengths?

Why not use the assessments to help parents predict how their children will likely do?

That's exactly what this book seeks to accomplish. By offering questionnaires on key factors known to predict parenting outcomes and children's development, similar to the ones that I administer to the parents in my research studies every day, parents can learn more about what kind of parent they are.

However, this book is not meant to be the last word on a given person's parenting or how his or her children will turn out. The information included here is necessarily based on statistical probabilities, just like my research on parenting and child development is. Yet I still hope you will gain insight into your parenting by taking the self-surveys, and that the book answers for you this question: What kind of parent am I?

Introduction

> It is easier to build strong children than to repair broken men.
> — Frederick Douglass

Standing at the tall silver swing set in the middle of the park, Marsha absent-mindedly pushes Gemma, her smiling toddler, on the baby swing. She watches Gemma giggling and gurgling as she swings back and forth with two chubby fingers in her drooling mouth. Her cheeks are rosy red.

She's happy despite all that teething, Marsha observes. Two older children break into Marsha's thoughts as they join Gemma on the swings, laughing and talking excitedly. The swings' chains jangle brightly as they mount the seats, the chime adding to the cheerful chorus of mid-summer. Marsha smiles. She wishes she could find as much joy in a simple swing.

Another child draws Marsha's attention. Wearing nothing but a sailor shirt and diaper, the little boy appears to have toddled off alone at the park. Marsha wonders where his parents might be. She watches as the toddler leans over, trying awkwardly to swing a chubby leg up on the teeter-totter. Undaunted, he skips over the sand toward the slide until the laughter of the children on the swings draws his attention. A big grin spreads across his face. He makes a beeline for the empty swing between Gemma and the older children.

Marsha's gaze snaps from the toddler to the older children on the swings. *They're going to smash right into him,* she thinks. She opens her mouth to call out but can't produce a sound. Her arms move with the tor- turous sluggishness of nightmares. Everything's going too fast. Her stomach clenches, as if bracing for impact on the young boy's behalf.

"Ian!" calls a voice from the far end of the play- ground. "There you are. Come to Grandma!"

The small boy stops a foot short of the swing's parabolic arc, oblivious to the feet whizzing through space that had nearly made contact with his head. He runs giggling to his grandma, who scoops him up. Ian squirms contentedly in his grandma's arms as she walks over to Marsha. Grandma adjusts his weight on her hip, moving him out of reach of Gemma's swing's gently swaying chain, to which Ian's fingers are inevitably drawn. Gemma observes the assemblage, fingers in her mouth.

Struggling slightly to contain the tyke, Grandma says, "I could see you were about to help. Thank you so much. I was just distracted for a moment by his brother. You must wonder what kind of grandparent I am to let my little one run off! It only takes a second!"

"No, not at all," Marsha murmurs and smiles in reassurance. "I know how quick these ones can be!"

WHO IS THIS BOOK FOR?

Has something like this scene played out for you before? Have you ever wondered what kind of parent you are? If you have, this book is for you. In this chapter I describe who I think will enjoy this book, and I hope you will see yourself reflected in that description.

First, I think this book is for parents, particularly those with younger children. What makes a "good parent"? Much has been written on the subject, drawing advice from philosophy, neurobiology, religious teachings, or personal experience. Authors of parenting books often assume that all parents will follow or respond to their advice in the same way. The truth is much more complex. Put simply, we usually parent the way we were parented. The decisions we make, the challenges we face, and the doubts, hopes, and desires we feel — all of these factors are drawn in part from how we were raised, and will leave lasting marks on our children's malleable minds. If we remain unaware of these influences, even the most well-meaning parents may slip back into old patterns, the latest research crumbling in the face of a deeply imbedded reflex.

It is here that my book is different. *What Kind of Parent Am I?* relies on clinically tested questionnaires (sometimes called surveys) and expert questioning to identify areas where parents may have the most trouble and, based on their responses, directs them to the appropriate passages in the book. This can be done by self-scoring my specially selected questionnaires provided at the beginning of chapters 1 through 8.

This should be an excellent book for expectant parents and parents of infants, toddlers, preschoolers, elementary school-age children, and even teenagers. It is a great book for moms and dads alike, though sadly most of the research I am drawing from has been on mothers. However, in my view, moms and dads and other caregivers, too, can learn from the research reviewed in every chapter. The sections on social support and how you can get help with parenting in each chapter are relevant for anyone who cares about helping parents and their children.

This is also a great book for grandparents, aunts and uncles, and child-care providers of all types. It is is for anyone who wants to know more about their skills and abilities, and anyone interested in knowing more about themselves and what they need to be the best caregiver they can be. After all, as I have said many times over the course of my career, parents cannot give what they do not have. Anyone who expects caregivers to give the best possible care to children when they themselves are suffering is expecting too much.

In general, this book is also for parents and caregivers who wish to learn what they need to do to help them overcome the stressors that can inhibit their ability to be nurturing and attentive. However, even if you think everything is going great and you just want to find out what kind of parent you are, this book is for you. I hope that I will be able to reassure many of you that you are truly doing a terrific job and that you have nothing to worry about as a parent. (I will use the word *parent* throughout this book, but by that I mean anyone who has responsibility for the regular care of children.)

Finally, this book is for anyone who wants to know about what factors are important for parents to function at their best. It is for parents who want to know how their weaknesses and strengths are linked to how successful their children are likely to be. It draws upon the latest science, including the new neuroscientific understanding of stress and how stress levels may affect both parents and children.

WHAT IS SO TOXIC ABOUT TOXIC STRESS?

This book is underpinned by the new neuroscience that has informed how we understand the impact of early environments on child development. Much of this has received attention in the media and has led many parents to conclude that their children need to lead stress-free lives. I disagree, because not all stress is bad.

Children's stress response systems are underdeveloped for the first years of their lives, and parents must therefore be the buffer against stress that their children do not yet possess. However, this does not mean that children should be coddled. In the following pages, I will outline the benefits of controlled, healthy levels of day-to-day stresses across a range of situations. Far from burdening the child, these brief and manageable episodes help calibrate children's responses to stress and are key in their development of patience, self-control, and emotional maturity.

The Center on the Developing Child at Harvard University describes three levels, or types, of stress called positive, tolerable, and toxic stress. When I talk of stress, typically I mean that the stress is experienced by parents and, through their reactions, trickles down to their children. Toxic stress is chronic, unrelenting stress and has the greatest consequences for children's physical, mental, and emotional development. Parents who suffer from depression or struggle with addiction provide typical examples. While the children in these families may not have a disorder, the experience of living in a household where such problems exist can be a toxic stressor to their development. Specifically, toxic stress triggers sustained activation of the hypothalamic-pituitary-adrenal axis (or HPA), which produces the stress hormone cortisol. At sustained, elevated doses, cortisol is neurotoxic — that is, it kills brain cells and may also negatively affect other body systems. Thus, this kind of toxic stress can interfere with healthy brain and organ development. (See my first book, *Scientific Parenting: What Science Reveals About Parental Influence*, for more details.)

Tolerable stress relates to stressors that are big, but short-lived. For example, a car accident can bring with it an intense burst of stress from fear or injury, but the effects of this stress can be mitigated and smoothed away over time. In the short-term, parents who experience tolerable stressors may become distracted, naturally, and find themselves responding inappropriately or ineffectively to their child's cues that signal needs. However, the short-lived nature of the stressor is less likely to affect children over the long-term and may even have positive side effects by encouraging resilience or teaching coping mechanisms. In this scenario, the HPA activation is not sustained, reducing potential damage to brain cells and organ systems.

Positive stress includes the minute frustrations or pangs of unease that each of us encounters every day. For most individuals, these incidents rack up as minor annoyances and can be handled easily and without help. Here, HPA activation is brief and the person is able to respond to and, ideally, successfully manage the stressor.

While the degree of a given stress — positive, tolerable, or toxic — has a big impact on how we react to it, the quality of a child's supportive relationships is significant. Nurturing, supportive relationships between children and their parents, extended family, or wider community can buffer the impact of moderate and high-level stressors. These supportive relationships can make tolerable or even toxic stress manageable. Positive stressors require little buffering, though even these can add up in the absence of supportive relationships.

In this book, levels of stressors are tied to each chapter's topic. For example, consider Chapter 8: Social Support and Co-Parenting. Social support is defined as the amount of help a person can expect to receive from their marital partner, family, friends, and other network members (for example, health-care providers) when they need it. Clearly, social support is not a stressor. However, a *lack* of social support is. For this reason, a strong network of social support would fall under the "low risk" heading, while little to no social support would be considered "high risk" or "toxic."

Chapters 1 through 8 will deal with the three levels of stress or risk, from positive (low) to toxic (high) levels, correlating with the categories defined by Harvard's Center on the Developing Child. For each level I offer solutions, practical tips, comfort, reassurance, and guidance to parents. For example, in Chapter 2: Serve and Return Parenting, I will explain how to nurture a strong and sustained parent–child relationship, especially for parents who score in the moderate or high level of stress range.

While stress is a necessary and even healthy component of our day-to-day lives, too much stress is bad for parents and their children. In 2012, the American Academy of Pediatrics issued an urgent call to action over the danger that severe and chronic stressful experiences — the toxic stressors — pose to children. Toxic stress in childhood can lead to all sorts of problems in adulthood, including depression, alcoholism, obesity, violent behaviour, heart disease, and even cancer. Though more common on the social margins, toxic stress can occur in any home, rich or poor, educated or not.

Perhaps the most important underpinning of this book is the following point: In my opinion, one of the few things that can consistently prevent stress from being toxic to children's health and development is supportive parenting. This is especially true in infancy and early childhood. Children's stress response systems are underdeveloped at birth; until they can function on their own, parents need to fill that role. Supportive parents, who are sensitive, responsive, and adaptable, do this job well and can insulate their children from all but the biggest catastrophes. Parents who are less sensitive, less attentive, or who regularly misinterpret their children's needs can let too much stress trickle through, or even cause it in the first place.

As children grow, other factors in the environment figure more prominently in helping to buffer the impact of toxic stressors on children; however, an excellent early foundation for children's resilience can still be found in the quality of relationships that children have with their parents, and that is where I want to focus.

WHY DO WE CARE ABOUT HOW WE PARENT? INTERGENERATIONAL PATTERNS

Caring about how we parent says something about us. It says we care enough about our children to be the kind of parent they need. This is an important point, as each child within a given family experiences his or her parents differently. Stressors come and go and two children in the same household can have very different experiences. (For a discussion of genetic susceptibility to environmental exposures, check out my first book, *Scientific Parenting*.) But overall, taking the time and expending the energy to figure out the best way to raise each child to meet his or her potential and individual needs has important intergenerational consequences.

The new science of epigenetics has shown us that experience changes how our genes express themselves and that this experience may be transferred to the next generation. In mice models[1,2] we see that stress in a great-great grandmother can be reflected in her great-great grandchildren across a host of domains, from behavioural problems to cardiovascular disease. Conversely, the effects of stress from long ago appear to be reduced by enrichment, which is nurturing care along with greater opportunities for learning and play. (If you want to know more about epigenetics, check out my first book for that, too.)

Also, an important interplay exists between environment and experience in predicting how well children will develop in life. Genetically, some children are more biologically sensitive to environmental influences than others.[3] Some children are called genetic "dandelions" and seem to do well in spite of whatever parenting environment that surrounds them. Other children are exquisitely biologically sensitive and are called "orchids," as they either do very well (like a carefully tended orchid) in supportive, enriched parenting environments, or wither and fare poorly (as would an orchid under the care of a gardener lacking a green thumb) in, for example, abusive, neglectful environments. Noteworthy is that genetic orchid children can have different outcomes (from very positive to very negative) even though they share the same genes that make them biologically sensitive to parenting environment. This shows that what matters most to them is the parenting environment, not their genes. In contrast, while parenting environment may not matter as much to the genetic dandelion (at least to our knowledge to date), in my view, the gift of supportive parenting should be available to all children, orchid or not.

So, by reading this book, not only will you uncover the risks to your parenting and your children's development, which may be derived from your own history, you will also gain ideas about ways to overcome those risks. You will also learn about your strengths and how to build on those. Your children, grandchildren, and great-grandchildren will thank you.

HOW TO USE THIS BOOK

There are a couple of ways to use this book. First, you can, of course, just flip to the sections that interest you. You can do the questionnaires at the beginning of those chapters and read the information most relevant to you. Or you can read front to back and complete the questionnaires in chapters 1 through 8. The chapter questionnaires are short and none should take you more than ten minutes to complete. Your scores on the questionnaires will personalize the reading recommendations and guide you to the sections that are most relevant to you.

AN IMPORTANT NOTE ABOUT
STATISTICAL PROBABILITIES

The questionnaire scores will guide you to the sections on low-, moderate-, and high-risk for each of the parenting challenges discussed in chapters 1 through 8. I have created these low, moderate, and high-risk categories by grouping scores from the questionnaires into three levels. Sometimes the cut-offs for the score levels (low, moderate, or high risk) are based on established, extensively validated scores for the questionnaire, like the Center for Epidemiological Studies Depression Scale (CESD). Some of the chapter surveys are based on my experience with asking these questions in my research, and no real guidelines for cut-offs even exist. If cut-offs have not been established, I have chosen them based on my years of experience as a researcher and with the recognition that there is a range of possible parenting outcomes within certain scores.

Rigorous researchers would argue with me about this approach and I am the first to admit it is more pragmatic than robust. However, even the most rigorous research findings are based on statistical probabilities, never certainties. We can know, for example, that for every one-point increase in depression scores (ranging from 0 to 60 on the CESD), the chance that parents' ability to be sensitive to their children in everyday interactions diminishes by, say, five percent in a questionnaire designed to measure parental sensitivity. However, these are probabilities and relate to samples drawn from populations. While social scientists are comfortable with the overall direction of associations, the precise magnitude that parental sensitivity is reduced by a parent being depressed can vary largely between individuals.

This is important, as statistical probabilities, while good at findings trends and offering guidelines for prediction, can never capture a person with one hundred percent accuracy, and this is further compounded by other variables which might offset a given stressor. For example, an individual with depression who is surrounded by a highly supportive family may not fall into the high-risk group, even though their depression score alone might place them there. I have attempted to account for and discuss these other angles in each chapter, but please note that if the risk level you attained from your score does not resonate with you, do not fret. Read about the risk level above or below the one that pertains to you based on your score, and hopefully you will find the material that makes sense for you. Even with this qualifying statement in mind, I am comfortable saying that the risk level scores you attain in your questionnaires will help you assess yourself.

Chapter 1

Trauma History

It's not stress that kills us, it is our reaction to it.

— Hans Selye

Mary's three-year-old son, Giovanni, is running a fever. His nose is plugged, his ears ache, and he coughs through half the night, fracturing her sleep and his. She's tried cough syrup and children's ibuprofen, but the fever won't break — it dips with every dose only to rise again a few hours later. Worried at its persistence, she makes an appointment with their family doctor and is seen the next day.

After twenty minutes in the waiting room, listening to a chorus of coughs and moans and sneezes from the other children, Mary is called into the doctor's office.

The nurse ushers her inside and reviews Mary and Giovanni's family medical history. Then the nurse hands Mary a form to fill out while she takes Giovanni's temperature. Mary glances at the paper, puzzled.

"What's this?" she asks.

"It's called the Adverse Childhood Experiences survey," explains the nurse. "The questions are a little personal, but we are giving it to all our patients now because it can tell a lot about family history and future health risks."

Mary thumbs through the pages. She winces at some of the words, which seem to rise off the page and smack her. "I would never do any of this to Gio," she says, her voice icy.

The nurse places a hand on her arm and gives her a reassuring look. "Of course not. This is about your history, not his."

"Okay, but I'm not sick."

"These things have a way of coming out in strange ways. If we know about them, we can help to fix any problems before they arise." The nurse's eyes meet Mary's. "Nothing you answer goes on any sort of record. We just look at the final score. I promise, it can help."

Mary studies the paper, uncertain.

"It should only take a few minutes. Just go through and answer the best you can."

"Okay," Mary says, uncapping the pen. "Here goes."

THE ADVERSE CHILDHOOD EXPERIENCES SURVEY

The following survey is often given to parents to assess their level of childhood trauma and to make predictions about how that trauma will potentially affect them and their children in the form of toxic stress. Take the survey now and then see the end of the chapter for your results and recommended resources.

Adverse Childhood Experiences Survey

Prior to your eighteenth birthday

1. Did a parent or other adult in the household often or very often swear at you, insult you, put you down, or humiliate you or act in a way that made you feel afraid you might be physically hurt?

If no, score 0 _____

If yes, score 1 _____

2. Did a parent or other adult in the household often or very often push, grab, slap, or throw something at you or ever hit you so hard that you had marks or were injured?

If no, score 0 _____

If yes, score 1 _____

3. Did an adult or person at least five years older than you ever touch or fondle you; have you touch their body in a sexual way; or attempt to have or actually have oral, anal, or vaginal intercourse with you?

If no, score 0 _____

If yes, score 1 _____

4. Did you often or very often feel that no one in your family loved you, or thought you were important or special, or that your family did not look out for each other, feel close to each other, or support each other?

If no, score 0 _____

If yes, score 1 _____

5. Did you often or very often feel that you did not have enough to eat, had to wear dirty clothes, and had no one to protect you or that your parents were too drunk or high to take care of you or take you to the doctor if you needed it?

If no, score 0 _____

If yes, score 1 _____

6. Were your parents ever separated or divorced?

If no, score 0 _____

If yes, score 1 _____

7. Was your mother or stepmother often or very often pushed, grabbed, slapped, or had something thrown at her; or sometimes, often, or very often kicked, bitten, hit with a fist, or hit with something hard; or ever repeatedly hit, over at least a few minutes, or threatened with a gun or knife?

If no, score 0 _____

If yes, score 1 _____

8. Did you live with anyone who was a problem drinker or alcoholic or who used street drugs?

If no, score 0 _____

If yes, score 1 _____

9. Was a household member depressed or mentally ill or did a household member attempt suicide?

If no, score 0 _____

If yes, score 1 _____

10. Did a household member go to prison?

If no, score 0 _____

If yes, score 1 _____

Now add up your "yes" answers.

This is your ACE score: _____

ACE score of 0: read *low risk*

ACE score of 1–3: read *moderate risk*

ACE score of 4+: read *high risk*

ABOUT TRAUMA AND PARENTING

This chapter focuses on the results of the Adverse Childhood Experiences (ACE) survey and on how parents' own trauma history threatens to bleed through into their children's lives. The landmark ACE study, conducted in San Diego, California, in 1995–1997, gathered data on the early life experiences and current mental and physical health status of over seventeen thousand middle-class adults. (This study is covered in more detail in *Scientific Parenting*.) Since then, a lot of research has focused on how the number of adverse experiences an adult undergoes before the age of eighteen can, with surprising accuracy, predict his or her likelihood of having many mental and physical health problems later in life. Results from the ACE survey provide us with a glimpse of the cumulative stress a given person experienced in childhood and distills that stress into a numeric measure of long-term risk. First, I will review the ACE research, then provide information relevant to your score for each of three levels of risk (low, moderate, and high).

ACEs are divided into three categories: a) childhood abuse, including emotional, physical, and sexual; b) neglect, including emotional and physical; and c) household dysfunction, including parental substance abuse, domestic violence, mental illness, criminal behaviour, and parental separation or divorce. Exposure to these influences as a child or teenager affects emotional, behavioural, cognitive, and social development, and even physical health in adulthood. What this means is that how *you* were parented or the adversity you experienced in the course of *your* earliest relationships with your parents has a lot to do with your health and how you parent your children today.

The ACE studies showed how pervasive ACEs are in the American population — more than half of participants (sixty-four percent) reported exposure to at least one type of adversity in childhood and twelve percent reported at least four types of exposure. Most people were exposed to more than one type of adversity, highlighting how ACEs often occur together. Research in other countries, including Canada, in the Alberta Adverse Childhood Experiences survey, the American National Comorbidity survey, and a New Zealand community survey,[4] showed that these findings held in other groups.

What is so compelling about ACE scores is their ability to accurately predict a wide array of issues, including psychosocial problems like adolescent pregnancy; unintended pregnancy in adult women; domestic violence in adult relationships; depression and suicide attempts;[5,6] health-risk behaviours like smoking, alcohol abuse, high-risk sexual behavior, and sexually transmitted diseases;[7] and even physical ailments like lung disease,[8] heart disease,[9] cancer, chronic pain, and allergies.[10]

Interestingly, ACEs appear to cluster more frequently in women than in men. The original ACE study found that 20.8 percent of women reported exposure to three or more ACEs, while only 14 percent of men reported the same. With the exception of physical abuse, every type of ACE was more prevalent in women than men. Moreover, ACEs affect women and men differently. Exposed to the same ACE, a woman is twice as likely as a man to exhibit depression.[11] The ACEs most often linked to poor mental health in adulthood are childhood physical abuse,[12] sexual abuse,[13] emotional abuse,[14] neglect,[15] and household dysfunction.[16] Emotional abuse is more strongly associated with depression than other type of childhood abuse. Exposure to psychological or emotional abuse encourages the formation and maintenance of negative perceptions and thought processes that can increase the onset and persistence of depression.[17]

There is also a strong "dose–response" relationship between ACEs and adult depression, meaning that the risk of negative outcomes rises along with the number of ACEs a person experiences. Women who reported five or more types of ACEs were 4.4 times more likely to suffer from depression in adulthood than women who reported no ACEs,[18] while each ACE added to a person's score increased their risk of attempted suicide two to five times.[19] Consequently, people who report multiple types of adversity may be at greater risk for the development of depression than those who report fewer adversities.

How you score on the ACE survey can predict your parenting behaviour. This is perhaps not surprising, as the poor health outcomes mentioned above can interfere with parents' ability to be emotionally present for their young children. Having a chronic disease such as a heart condition can reduce the energy it takes to adequately attend to children's needs on a daily basis. Higher ACE scores can also translate into more risk-taking behaviours among parents as well, which come with additional consequences for children. In one study, pregnant women who had higher ACE scores were more likely to smoke cigarettes or use recreational drugs during pregnancy,[20] which can impact the health of the developing fetus.

Higher ACE scores can also indicate an increased risk of postpartum depression.[21] Having more ACEs also predicted adults' unresolved states of mind;[22] that is, unresolved trauma about childhood experiences, which is thought to interfere with parenting. ACEs also predict an increased likelihood of violence between marital partners,[23] and my own research shows that family violence is a potent predictor of problems in children's development across a range of domains. Other Canadian researchers — Howard and Miriam Steele and their team at the New School of New York — also found that parents with higher ACE scores were more likely to find parenthood stressful, to cite dysfunctional interactions with their children, and to perceive their child as difficult.

ACEs in one generation are also known to affect children's development directly in the next. Specific ACEs experienced by parents as children, such as experiencing violence between their parents[24] or being abused as a child,[25] are linked to behavioural problems in children in the next generation. Mothers' histories of childhood abuse directly predicted socioemotional problems in their six-month-old infants — they were perceived as more difficult, smiling less often, having difficulty calming down, having trouble feeding, and crying excessively.[26] Similarly, an additional study found that more maternal ACEs were associated with increased emotional health difficulties in eighteen-month-old infants.[27] In a study of preschoolers, mothers' ACE scores were positively associated with more child behavioural problems, including anxiety, depression, aggressive behaviour, attention problems, and overall worse scores for internalizing (for example, anxiety) and externalizing (aggression, hyperactivity) behavioural problems.[28] (While compelling, mothers in this sample also reported being abused by their marital partners.) My own research has recently revealed that mothers' ACE scores predicted more anxiety and hyperactive behaviours in their twenty-four month old toddlers, especially when mothers were very depressed or anxious during pregnancy or the early postpartum period. Boys demonstrated the greatest vulnerability to both high maternal ACE scores and perinatal depression and anxiety.

It is clear that the ACEs parents experienced as children can impact how they cope with their parenting responsibilities, potentially affecting the next generation. See below for a summary of each risk category and find out which one matches your score.

SCORES ON THE ACE SURVEY

Low Risk (Score: 0)

If you scored 0 ACEs, congratulations! You are one of the lucky approximately thirty percent of the population that have this kind of idyllic childhood. Read on or go to the next chapter's questionnaire.

In the first scenario, Mary attained 0.

Moderate Risk (Score: 1–3)

If you scored 1 to 3 on the ACE survey, first think about whether the experience you had still affects you today. Are you depressed or do you have other mental health or relationship challenges? Do you have health problems? Are they possibly linked to your earlier childhood experiences? Not all of the problems adults face are due to their childhood traumas. Like the dandelion children, many people are resilient in spite of their exposure to early adversity, so this could be you.

However, if you do feel affected by your early adversity, there are solutions. In recent years, research has shown that adverse early experiences and even day-to-day stressors are manageable with supportive relationships. I encourage you to read Chapter 8: Social Support and Co-Parenting to learn whether you are well-supported, and to explore ways of building your support network, which is essential.

If you have mental health conditions, attending to your mental health is paramount. See your family physician or nurse practitioner and ask for a referral to supportive psychological counselling. It may be helpful to discuss your family history of ACEs and how they may contribute to the mental health concerns affecting your life today. If you are in an abusive relationship, often linked to exposure to early ACEs, refer to Chapter 6: Abuse and Violence. Most health professionals have heard of ACEs and sharing your score may be a helpful way of beginning the discussion. You can also refer to Chapter 4: Depression, Chapter 8: Social Support and Co-Parenting, and Chapter 2: Serve and Return Parenting, which may offer you more insight.

Three ACEs. Mary flips back to the instructions and double-checks her answers, ensuring she didn't make a mistake somewhere. It all adds up. One, two, three.

Her first reaction is shock — she doesn't think of herself as a victim, as someone damaged by childhood trauma. But as she reads back over the questions and reflects on what they ask her, it begins to make more sense, because there *were* dark days, for a time. She remembers what her childhood was like, shortly after the divorce. Her mom's nightly glass of rum and Coke grew to two, then three, and the bottles piled up in the recycling, their long necks pointing like accusing fingers in every direction. She remembers when the afternoons stretched into protracted innings of some crude contact sport, a game called "Don't Make Mom Mad." She and her brother were reluctant participants with an incomplete grasp of the rules. She also remembers when the smacks brightened her cheeks — never closed-fisted, never hard enough to bruise, with a sting that lingered in the gut long after the pain on her skin subsided.

How horrible it seems, looking back on it. But at the time it had just been life, and there'd been good times to balance out the bad: weekends with her dad and stepmother Carol, a friendly woman with the bubbly aura of a big sister; sleepovers with friends, bingeing on chocolate and bad horror movies; days when the glasses of rum and Coke ceased their merciless multiplication. The good times grew more frequent as time went on, and eventually her mother quit drinking altogether.

The nurse looks at the final score and sits down next to Mary.

"Is it bad?" Mary asks.

"That's for you to tell me," says the nurse. "Do you think your past experiences have affected you in any way? Are they something you think about as a parent?"

Mary bites her lip. She knows she would never hit Giovanni. The very thought of it repulses her. It's hard enough for her to raise her voice, even when Giovanni misbehaves or does something dangerous, like the time she caught him trying to pry the safety cover off of the electrical outlet.

And then there's the anxiety that creeps in sometimes from the corners of her mind, a gradual tightening of the belly until it can feel difficult to breathe. It was a problem in her early twenties, but things had gotten better since she married Antonio. He's a constant support, and with him in her corner, her anxiety's grip has lost much of its strength. She doesn't drink and neither does he — the two of them even turn down the inevitable glass of red wine offered by her Italian in-laws.

"I guess they have," says Mary. "But not so I can't deal with them." She puts the clipboard aside and extends her arms, welcoming Giovanni as he crawls eagerly into her lap.

High Risk (Score: 4 or More)

If you experienced four or more stressors, it is likely that your upbringing has, to some extent, impacted your mental or physical health. However, as with any toxic stressor, the quality of support you receive from your adult relationships plays a large role in whether or not these life experiences transfer to your relationships with your children.

Remember: Stressors are only toxic in the absence of supportive relationships. Do you feel supported? Do you have people to step in when you are not functioning your best? Do you have a partner you can count on? Do you have friends or family members you can turn to in times of need? These support systems can serve as an important buffer, smoothing out the jagged edges that ACEs might otherwise inflict. So rest assured, the effects of these experiences are not irreversible or even assured. You can flip to chapter 8 to discover how well you are supported and to get advice about how to reach out.

As indicated in the Moderate Risk section, it is still possible that you are doing well despite your exposure to adversity. You could be what social scientists refer to as "resilient," meaning that you have been successful in spite of the risks you experienced. If you do not have any concerns that you would attribute to your high ACE score, you are, by definition, resilient. If this is you, congratulations! You are a marvel.

However, there are many factors that can explain or build resilience. As suggested above, supportive relationships can make a significant difference, especially when encountered early in life. In a famous study conducted in Kauai, Hawaii, researchers selected nearly two thousand children exposed to high levels of adversity and followed them into adulthood. They found that one of the most potent predictors of resilient adults was the presence of a supportive, nurturing adult, and the person did not have to be the child's parent. The resilient adults from the Kauai study reported that someone special had cared for them as children and over time. If you have had a caregiver like this in your life, this person could have made the difference for you.

A healthy, loving relationship with your partner today can also make the difference, as can intelligence.[29] Much as you can buffer the impact of toxic stress on your child, having a supportive loving partner can buffer the impacts of *your* current and past stress on *you*. Intelligence can also make a difference, likely because intelligent people can think about their own needs and find resources to help them overcome stress or even imagine and plan a different life into their future.

If you are struggling with health problems, especially mental health conditions such as depression, then attending to your well-being is paramount. Your efforts will help not just yourself but also your children, since a healthy parent is much more likely to be an attentive parent. As suggested above, find the resources you could benefit from. Ask your family doctor or nurse practitioner for a referral to supportive psychological counselling. Discuss your family history and how it may have contributed to the mental health concerns affecting your life today. Most health professionals have now heard of ACEs, and sharing your score may be a helpful way of starting the discussion. Work with a counsellor who can assess whether you have unresolved trauma with respect to your early experiences. Attending to unresolved issues could have positive consequences in other areas, such as reducing parenting stress. So do not delay — attending to your needs may be the best gift you give yourself and your child.

Several chapters in this book will help you gain insight into your situation. But, by far, and it deserves repeating, the biggest sources of resilience in spite of the risks you have been exposed to are the social support you can attain from others. If you are having relationship challenges, you can refer to Chapter 8: Social Support and Co-Parenting or Chapter 6: Abuse and Violence, or if you are having parenting challenges, you can refer to Chapter 2: Serve and Return Parenting. These chapters will offer you more insight.

Many books are available on the subject of Adverse Childhood Experiences that may be helpful for you, too. These include

- *The ACEs Revolution! The Impact of Adverse Childhood Experiences* by John Trayser
- *Childhood Disrupted: How Your Biography Becomes Your Biology and How You Can Heal* by Donna Nakazawa
- *The Deepest Well: Healing the Long-Term Effects of Childhood Adversity* by Nadine Burke Harris

Nadine Burke Harris also has a great TED talk on ACEs, which you can find at www.ted.com/talks/nadine_burke_harris_how_childhood_trauma_affects_health_across_a_lifetime.

Whatever you do, do not despair! The fact that so many people are resilient despite the risks they experienced early on is evidence that you can be resilient, too. You just may need a little help.

Six. The number glares up at Mary from the page like an accusing eye. Six ACEs. She feels numb from the neck down, though beneath the shock rumbles a righteous anger, a vindication that the events of her childhood, for so long repressed and downplayed as the inevitable hiccups of a rocky but typical upbringing, were actually worth getting upset about.

The first thing she recalls is the divorce — a household torn down the middle. It had been a rough one, with lawyers neither party could afford unleashed on both sides, leaving little to fight over but a few meagre scraps and a run-down house mortgaged to the rafters.

Next came her mother's drinking. The glasses strewn over every surface, their bottoms sticky with the residue of rum and Coke. The recycling bins full of empty bottles that rattled like bones whenever the garage door opened. The punishments oscillated wildly in severity from day-to-day, where breadcrumbs on the counter might earn a smack across the cheek, while a blown curfew garnered an indulgent shrug.

After that was Cheryl, her father's second wife, whose youth and kindness inverted the fairy tale trope: no wicked stepmother here; it was her biological mother who turned cruel. She'd stopped hitting Mary by then, but her tongue could cause far deeper wounds. Any mention of Cheryl unsheathed its ruthless edge.

And then there was Kevin. Smirking, ubercool Kevin, with his blond hair stylishly mussed and his jeans artfully torn. He'd had a cooing charm that tempered his bad boy wardrobe, conjuring inexplicable trust from parents who should have taken one look at him and scoffed. He won them over by cutting lawns and delivering papers — he was an industrious worker who got the news to every door on time and never failed to mow an awkward fringe of grass. Mary's mother, impressed, had hired him to babysit when Mary was nine. He'd been fun enough until after supper, when he led her to the bathroom and pulled down his pants.

"Here, look at this," he said. "Now show me yours."

Somehow Mary relates this to the nurse without crying. She tells the nurse about her recurrent battle with depression over the years. It's Giovanni who stays her tears, knowing that he could never understand — that she never wants him to understand — how deeply she hurt.

"Have you ever spoken to anyone about this?" the nurse asks, holding Mary's hand in hers. Mary nods.

"Shrinks, for a while, when I was a teenager. They got me on antidepressants. The pills made things a bit easier, and eventually I got sick of talking about it so I just stopped going. That was a few years ago," she adds, realizing as she speaks that it was actually more than a decade.

"It may be worth thinking about going back. Do you have anyone to help out at home? Siblings, maybe, or friends who live nearby?" The nurse knows better than to ask about Giovanni's father. Antonio left two years ago. He'd approached her depression like a mechanic sizing up a dodgy engine, prodding and tinkering, trying fix after fix, until throwing up his hands he declared the whole car totalled.

Mary nods. "My brother helps out a lot. And I get some money from my mom. Things got a lot better with her after she quit drinking."

"That's good." The nurse lists a few more services Mary could draw on in her community: group counselling sessions, support groups, churches. Though the nurse never mentions money, Mary is grateful to note that she lists things that are free or charge on a sliding scale. They wrap up the discussion and the nurse leaves. The doctor comes in a few minutes later and, after a few simple questions and a peek in Giovanni's ear, writes a prescription for antibiotics.

"There," he says. "I hope this sorts everything out for you."

"I hope so, too," Mary says.

Chapter 2

Serve and Return Parenting

There are times as a parent when you realize that your job is not to be the parent you always imagined you would be, the parent you always wished you had. Your job is to be the parent your child needs, given the particulars of his or her own life and nature.

— Ayelet Waldman

The lights in the playroom switch off and on. The attendant claps her hands in a simple beat and begins to sing: "Clean up, clean up, everybody everywhere! Clean up, clean up, everybody do your share!" A dozen children and their parents heed the call, clearing scaled-down tables covered with plastic fruit, and tossing foam blocks into baskets. Lila watches with pride — and a bit of amusement, if she's being honest — as Brooklyn staggers beneath a swaying tower of stuffed animals, keen to drop them into their appointed cubby in a single dramatic swoop. She mostly makes it, spilling a few in the process, which Lila picks up and puts beside the rest.

"Good job, B. Now let's get going."

"Can't we stay for circle time?" asks Brooklyn.

"Not today, sweetie. Mommy's got to go home and get lunch started. Another time."

Brooklyn gives a showy pout but leaves without further prompting, and is skipping again by the time they reach the entrance hall. A bulletin board hangs from one wall, and as they walk by a colourful notice catches Lila's eye:

How is YOUR child developing?

Our research team is conducting a study on how parenting affects children's development and health.

Do you have a child between the ages of 3 and 5? If so, we want to hear from you!

At the bottom of the form dangles a series of perforated strips containing the study lead's contact information. On a whim, Lila grabs one and tucks it into her wallet. She had studied psychology in university and likes the idea of helping grad students the same way her own participants had helped her.

At home, Lila fixes lunch and helps Brooklyn with her colouring. Once Brooklyn is down for her nap, Lila fishes out the contact slip and sends an email to the listed address, asking for more information. She receives a reply fifteen minutes later thanking her for her interest. The study, the email explains, aims to examine predictors of health among preschool children. To participate, Lila would need to sit for an interview, which could take place by telephone. Lila writes back saying she'd be happy to take part and lists a few times that work for her.

A few weeks later, Lila receives a telephone call.

"Hello?"

"Hello, is this Ms. Lila Foster?" asks a voice on the other end of the line.

"Speaking."

"Hi, Ms. Foster. My name's Dan and I'm with Dr. Motes' research team. A few weeks back you agreed to participate in a brief telephone interview with us. Are you still interested?"

"Sure," Lila says.

After a long preamble about Lila's rights as a study participant, the interviewer begins asking her a series of questions.

SERVE AND RETURN SURVEY

The following survey is like many used in research studies to assess how parenting behaviours affect children's development and health. Take the survey and then see the end of the chapter for your results and recommended resources.

Serve and Return Survey

How often do you

1. Praise your child by saying something like "Good for you!" or "What a nice thing you did!" or "That's good going!"?

SCORE	Never	About once a week or less	A few times a week	One or two times a day	Many times each day
	0	1	2	3	4

2. Talk or play with your child, focusing attention on each other for five minutes or more, just for fun?

SCORE	Never	About once a week or less	A few times a week	One or two times a day	Many times each day
	0	1	2	3	4

3. Laugh with your child?

SCORE	Never	About once a week or less	A few times a week	One or two times a day	Many times each day
	0	1	2	3	4

4. Do something special with your child that he/she enjoys like games, hobbies, sports, outings, or other enjoyable activities?

SCORE	Never	About once a week or less	A few times a week	One or two times a day	Many times each day
	0	1	2	3	4

5. Respond to your child's signals that they need something from you?

SCORE	Never	About once a week or less	A few times a week	One or two times a day	Many times each day
	0	1	2	3	4

Tally scores from each row:

Score 9–20: read *low risk*

Score 1–8: read *moderate risk*

Score 0: read *high risk*

PARENTING MEANS PAYING ATTENTION, NOTICING, AND RESPONDING

This chapter focuses on how a set of parenting behaviours can make a tremendous difference in children's capacity to grow and succeed in life. These behaviours, called "serve and return" by the Harvard Center on the Developing Child, are a group of high-quality parent–infant interactions that have been found to support and predict children's optimal health and development.

Serve and return is a metaphor easily understood by those who play tennis or other games that require the "serve" of a ball, for example, and a "return" of the ball. Two people take part in the "game" or interaction; the child is understood in this metaphor to offer up the serves, and the parent is responsible for paying attention to the serve and appropriately returning the serve, so that the child and parent can continue the game or interaction.

In a serve and return relationship, then, the child offers up a series of cues — or serves — signalling their interests, moods, or desires. These cues might be laughing at something they see, staring keenly at an object, or asking a question about something they have experienced. The parent then responds in a manner that addresses the child's interest, returning the serve and, in the process, building a stronger bond with the child.

The returns can vary greatly depending on the situation and the child's age, including back-and-forth babbling (for infants), talking together (for older children), or taking part in games, hobbies, or other activities that the child enjoys. Praise is also a valuable way to build a serve and return relationship, as it shows the child that their parent is focused on them. More subtle examples include parents noticing that their child

- is tired, so they make arrangements for the child to nap or go to bed for the night;
- is afraid of something (for example, a dog), so they comfort the child until he or she is emboldened (in this case, to safely pat the dog);
- needs a break from an activity, so they change the pace or activity according to how the child signals their interest with various serves; and
- is easily frustrated by normally neutral activities (for example, getting ready for school), so they make gentle inquiries about the source of frustration or irritation.

As its name implies, a serve and return relationship requires active engagement on both sides. Children need to do their part by responding to their parent in turn. Shared laughter is a great example of a fruitful two-way exchange, as it reflects a deeper connection and draws parent and child closer together. Of course, the "shared" aspect of laughter is critical; laughter a child feels is at their expense would have quite the opposite effect.

Healthy serve and return interactions are characterized by parental sensitivity and responsiveness. Sensitive, responsive interactions convey warmth, as opposed to coldness. Think of how unpleasant it is to get the "cold shoulder."

At any age, the cold shoulder is associated with feelings of rejection and being disliked. Warm interactions deliver the opposite sensation: inclusion instead of exclusion, acceptance rather than rejection. In relationships built on sensitivity and responsiveness, the parent and child enjoy each other's company, and it shows in their smiling, eye contact, touching, and attentive, spontaneous conversations. Healthy serve and return interactions are also referred to as being "contingently responsive." Contingency refers to the timing of the serves and returns, as waiting too long to respond to a child's cue negates the benefit of the interaction. As in tennis, a serve must be returned promptly; otherwise, the ball inevitably bounces out of bounds, and the parent "misses the point."

Serve and return interactions also lead to secure parent–child attachment, a term that refers to the way in which a child interacts with the world beyond their parents and copes with brief episodes of separation. In other words, the child whose parent has regularly paid attention to his or her serves by returning them with helpful responses develops not only a solid serve and return relationship, but also is likely to have a secure parent–child attachment.

The quality of parent–child attachment may be secure (considered the healthiest) or insecure. Securely attached children are confident and outgoing, happily exploring the world around them and returning to their parents briefly for occasional check-ins. Securely attached children are more likely to use their parents as a secure base and safe haven for exploring their environments than insecurely attached ones.[30] Secure attachment is associated with many positive outcomes over the lifespan, including

- socioemotional adjustment
- reduced anxiety
- better relationships with school-age peers
- reduced delinquency, aggression, and conduct disorder[31-33]
- higher intelligence and language skills[34]
- reduced rates of all types of physical illness, including inflammatory health conditions such as cardiovascular disease.[35]

Strong serve and return relationships foster secure parent–child attachment by helping children develop a feeling of confidence that their parent can be relied upon now and in the future to ensure the child's safety. These children confidently explore the environment, playing with toys and engaging with people like relatives and peers and with other aspects of the environment, knowing that their parents will be there if they need them.

In contrast, insecure attachment patterns with parents (the most severe being "disorganized attachment") are linked to children's

- aggression
- behavioural problems
- antisocial behaviour
- anxiety
- depression.

In young adults, suicidality and depression have been linked to poor attachment with parents in childhood.

(For more information on attachment, refer to *Scientific Parenting*.)

Not surprisingly, the more an infant or child explores their environment, the better their cognitive and social skills develop. Research abounds showing that early parent–child experiences characterized by healthy serve and return interactions are linked to children's later IQ and provide the model for future peer relationships into adulthood. Even children's resiliency to stress or their ability to cope with stressors is tied to healthy serve and return interactions.[36] My own research has found that serve and return relationships characterized by not enough parental responsiveness predicted inflammatory skin conditions, such as psoriasis or skin rash, in toddlers.

An extreme example of a lack of serve and return interactions was observed in the studies of Romanian institutionalized children, many of whom were adopted into Western countries such as the United States and Canada. The longer that children lived in these institutions, where nurturing interactions were all but non-existent and what little care they received came on a strict, non-contingent schedule, the worse their outcomes. A typical Romanian orphan was fed at a set time whether they were hungry or not, and diapers were changed whether they were wet or dry. Social interactions of any kind were discouraged. Neural images of these children displayed dramatically reduced brain sizes, and studies showed severely altered cognitive, social-emotional, and behavioural development. Happily, once adopted into warm and loving homes with healthy serve and return interactions, nearly all the children improved in functioning.

Attachment patterns established early in life tend to persist over time, unless dramatic changes (that is, ACEs) occur in the family. Since healthy serve and return interactions offer the greatest chance for establishing secure parent–infant attachment, it is important to understand and address the barriers.

WHAT INTERFERES WITH SERVE AND RETURN PARENTING?

A number of things can interfere with healthy serve and return interactions. For one thing, children must send clear cues about their needs and wants. Healthy serve and return is not all the parents' responsibility, because sometimes children are less able to communicate their interests. For example, babies born preterm are often easily overwhelmed by noise, lights, and other sensations; they shut down by sleeping excessively and are unable to interact due to fussiness. Baby colic, or excessive infant crying that is not easily soothed, also prevents healthy serve and return interactions between parents and children. Babies whose crying (that is, serves) cannot be soothed regardless of what parents might try — rocking, feeding, changing, singing lullabies — make a successful return all but impossible. Thankfully, babies outgrow these tendencies but they prove very challenging for parents in the early days nonetheless.

Parents in highly stressful situations have also been observed to display non-contingent interaction styles that interfere with serve and return. Research on mothers raising children in high-stress environments, such as households where the parents have low income (see Chapter 3: Socio-Economic Risk) or mental health problems (see Chapter 4: Depression), are less sensitive to babies' and children's serves because stressors and other challenges may be distracting and make it difficult to pay attention. They tend to be unrealistic in their expectations of baby and child behaviour and are impatient, which interferes with healthy serve and return interactions. They offer fewer returns by being less verbal and responsive to their children and are more prone to using physical punishment, an inappropriate return of the child's serve.[37]

SCORES ON THE SERVE AND RETURN SURVEY

A note about this questionnaire: It is very difficult to assess serve and return relationships between parents and children with questionnaires alone. The dozens of daily exchanges that comprise a healthy serve and return relationship can be tough to spot even for a trained observer. Asking parents to recall and record these interactions themselves presents an even greater challenge. In a research setting, investigators often assess the quality of serve and return relationships by video recording parents and children as they engage in various day-to-day activities, then tease apart the resulting videos to identify the quality and quantity of serve and return in the interactions.

With these limitations in mind, I encourage you to pay close attention to your child's cues, which signal their needs or wants for interaction, a break, or change. Consider your own responses and how the interaction plays out. Did the serve and return keep the game going? Or did you miss the serve? Or did the return miss the mark and end the game (interaction)?

This questionnaire alone may not sufficiently describe your serve and return relationship with your child. However, the questions posed provide a rough framework for understanding and assessing the behaviours that promote healthy serve and return relationships. My hope is that by completing the survey you will become more alert to your own actions and how they can improve your relationship with your child.

Low Risk (Score: 9–20)

If you scored between 9 and 20, congratulations — it is very likely that you have healthy serve and return interactions with your child or children. Remember to pay attention to how well you are able to identify your child's cues and ask yourself if your responses keep the "game" going with your child.

> Lila pokes her head out the door and fishes through the mailbox for the day's deliveries. She spots the envelope amongst the usual bills and junk mail. It stands out by its bulk and the official-looking crest printed on the front.

She knows immediately what it is and suddenly feels unexpectedly nervous as she tears open the envelope and scans its contents.

The package begins with a letter thanking her for her participation. After the letter comes a detailed report, which she skims, followed by an assessment of her serve and return relationship with Brooklyn. She scored 16 out of 20, putting her firmly in the low risk category. Smiling at the news, Lila sets the letter aside and returns to the playroom, where Brooklyn is putting the final pieces in her new puzzle.

Moderate Risk (Score: 1–8)

If you scored in the moderate risk range, this suggests that you might be missing prime opportunities for serve and return interactions with your child. Consider whether other stressors may be interfering with the quality of your serve and return interactions. Are you depressed? Do you need income support? Consider seeking out support for both your parenting concerns as well as other stressors that may be interfering. A good start is with your family physician or nurse practitioner. Local parenting programs are also excellent for offering tips and can help you with healthy serve and return interactions.

Making an effort to notice and respond in a timely way to the cues that signal need is an important place to start. Older children can tell you their needs, even if this takes coaxing, but with babies it is a bit more difficult. Yet many of babies' non-verbal cues are just like those of older children and adults and can tell you a lot. Examples of cues that signal your baby or child may need a break or a change include

- yawning, falling asleep
- coughing
- crawling or walking away
- fussing, crying
- averting gaze (eye contact followed by looking away)
- grimacing
- back arching
- dull-looking face or eyes
- holding the hand to ear or face.

Examples of cues that show your child wants to interact with you include

- babbling, talking
- raising brows
- gazing at your face
- relaxed fingers and hands
- giggling, laughing
- raising the head (as if interested)
- reaching toward you
- smiling.[38]

Some of these examples will seem obvious to you, but thinking about how they play out in interactions with babies compared to older children may be helpful. Also, trying to be present in the moment for your child and trying to consider what might be on his or her mind is a great place to start in improving your serve and return relationship. For tips on this, see Chapter 7: Reflective Function.

Other activities that may enhance your serve and return opportunities with babies include the following:

- massaging your baby
- singing songs or rhymes
- looking at picture books
- talking to your baby
- making eye contact
- holding your baby
- smiling at your baby
- playing games with your baby

For preschoolers, try these activities:

- reading stories or books together
- playing games
- doing crafts
- simple cooking together
- simple chores together
- exercising together
- eating meals together
- hugging your child
- making eye contact and smiling

And for school-age and older children, these activities may improve your serve and return opportunities:

- reading the books/watching the shows/engaging in the gaming they like and discussing them
- showing interest in their friends, interests, ideas, hobbies
- taking part in games, interests, and hobbies together
- cooking together
- building a project together
- engaging in household chores together
- doing sports together
- going to movies and talking about each other's perspectives
- play wrestling
- eating meals together
- hugging your child
- making eye contact and smiling

Lila flips through the report until she finds her results. She bites her lip. Moderate risk. She doesn't like the sound of that. It seems like a harsh pronouncement, though the more she considers it, the more she realizes that she really can get distracted quite a bit. There are always so many things to deal with in a day. It can be tough to pay as much attention to Brooklyn as she maybe should.

Near the back of the report, Lila spots a list of parenting resources. She notices a parenting class being held at the local YWCA. After a moment's pause, she punches the URL into her phone and signs up.

High Risk (Score: 0)

If you scored high risk, it is a good idea for you to speak about this with your family physician, nurse practitioner, or a registered nurse in your public health or community clinic. You should inquire about being referred for observational assessment of the quality of your serve and return relationship with your child. Specially trained nurses, social workers, psychologists, and psychiatrists can assess you and your child or children through many observational means. You may also benefit from infant–parent psychotherapy, family therapy, or parent–child interaction guidance from a counsellor, psychologist, or psychiatrist. If searching for a therapist online, try using the terms *infant mental health* or *child mental health* and the name of your town/city/region.

Unfortunately, not as many people are trained in these skills as there is need, so it may take a while to find the right person or the right resource. But do not give up — there are experts in most communities. In the meantime, join a parenting program, which will also be of help. Seek them out in your local community by searching online for parenting programs. Also, try search terms such as *parenting programs* or *parenting classes* and the name of your town/city/region. Some well-known programs include Circle of Security, Nurse-Family Partnership Program, Keys to Caregiving, and Triple P Parenting (triplep.net/glo-en/home). Searching for these programs in your community online may lead you to these or related resources.

There are also great resources online that explain the impact of serve and return interactions on your child, such as the Harvard Center on the Developing Child's video on serve and return (https://developingchild.harvard.edu/science/key-concepts/serve-and-return) and the Alberta Family Wellness Initiative's serve and return video (www.albertafamilywellness.org/resources/video/serve-and-return). I also recommend the book *The Art of Sensitive Parenting* by Katherine Kersey because it may help you to better tune in to your child's cues and give you guidance on how to respond to the full range of your child's behaviour. Be sure to refer to the list in the Moderate Risk section above, which gives examples of babies' and children's cues that signal the desire to continue, stop, or change the serve and return exchange. Also in the Moderate Risk section, see the list that offers suggestions for other activities that may enhance your serve and return opportunities with your child. Chapter 7: Reflective Function may also help with serve and return relationships by helping attune you to what may be on your child's mind, which underpins your child's cue or signal to you.

Most importantly, consider every moment with your child as an opportunity to engage in a pleasant serve and return interaction. Diaper changes, bath time, chores, cooking together, meal time, and even driving in the car together all provide opportunities — try to take advantage of all of them. But do not beat yourself up if you miss opportunities from time to time because you are distracted. Making an effort most of the time is what is important. And with older children, to extend the metaphor, if you know the "ball" was dropped in your serve and return relationship, you can even have a conversation about it and try to repair and restart the game with your child.

However, if some stressor (for example, depression or low income) is impacting on your life and is regularly interfering with your ability to have healthy serve and return interactions with your child, it should be addressed. Please refer to the appropriate chapters for other risk factors that may be interfering with the quality of the serve and return relationship you have with your child. Also be sure to refer to Chapter 8: Social Support and Co-Parenting for tips on building strengths in your adult relationships that can aid you in developing an optimal serve and return relationship.

Lila's hand trembles slightly. The letter crumples at the corner where her fingers grip it tight. Her eyes circle around the same words over and over again: "concern about Brooklyn's performance." She sets the letter down and rubs her temples. What has she been doing wrong? She can be busy, sure, but she'd always thought she was an attentive parent. After a moment she picks the letter back up and continues reading the assessment. The research lead suggests several resources and provides a number she can call if she has questions. With a sniff, she unlocks her phone and begins dialling the number.

Chapter 3

Socio-Economic Risk

We think sometimes that poverty is only being hungry, naked and homeless. The poverty of being unwanted, unloved and uncared for is the greatest poverty. We must start in our own homes to remedy this kind of poverty.

— Mother Theresa

Mary opens her web banking page and sighs. The black and red lines that represent her account balance and outstanding debt engage in the latest clash of their constant battle, and this time red appears to have the edge.

She looks through her credit card statements to find the one due soonest and tosses a heap of cash at it before the late fees can sink their fangs into her. The other two cards eye her hungrily. She cues up a payment for the second one but pauses. Had this week's cheque for Giovanni's daycare gone out already? It must have — why else would her account be so low. She double-checks and sees with dismay that the usual four-hundred-and-fifty dollar charge hasn't yet been levied, meaning her meagre balance is due to shrink even further within two days. With a sigh, she closes the browser while imagining the unsated credit cards hissing angrily at her negligence.

She hooks her thumbnail against her upper teeth and gnaws at it gently, not quite cracking the keratin. When had money gotten so tight? Antonio leaving didn't help, of course. And her job at the accounting firm pays the mortgage and puts food on the table, but its inadequacy grew more apparent with every passing week as a little more of each paycheque went to paying off debts from days or weeks before. Forget saving for the future; she could barely afford to save for the present.

Maybe she should get another job, something part-time that could bring in a few more dollars. But she gets little enough time with Giovanni as it is. Thinking of her son, she wonders how this strain feels to him. She hides the crunch from him as best she can, but he's a clever boy. Surely he knows something's the matter.

Opening a fresh browser tab, Mary types *Are my money problems affecting my child?* and hits enter. She finds a questionnaire that measures socio-economic status. Suspecting she won't like what she hears, she nevertheless begins completing the questionnaire.

THE SOCIO-ECONOMIC RISK SURVEY

The survey below is like many used in research studies to assess socio-economic status. Take the survey and then see the end of the chapter for your results and recommended resources.

Socio-Economic Risk Survey

1. Does your family income usually meet your basic needs for housing, food, clothing, and occasional leisure activity/entertainment (for example, movies or a night out)?

Yes (score 3) _____

No (score 0) _____

2. What is the highest level of schooling you completed (select one answer)?

Did not complete high school (score 0) _____

High school (score 1) _____

High school + vocational training (score 2) _____

Bachelor's degree (score 3) _____

Graduate or professional degree (score 4) _____

3. Are you married/common-law?

Yes (score 3) _____

No (score 0) _____

Total Score: _____

Score of 6–10: read *low risk*

Score of 3–5: read *moderate risk*

Score of 0–2: read *high risk*

IT IS NOT JUST ABOUT MONEY

This chapter focuses on the effects of socio-economic status (SES) on parenting risk. Despite the sound of its name, SES has less to do with parents' income than with their type of employment, quality of education, and marital status. Other important SES factors include family size, parental–occupation prestige, and eligibility for government subsidies.

In some ways, boys and girls are affected differently by low SES. Boys from low-SES families seem to be most vulnerable to externalizing problems,[39] which are behaviours that are directed outwardly toward the social environment and are characterized by under-controlled and outer-directed patterns of development such as hyperactivity or aggression. Girls, in general, tend to be more at risk of internalizing problems, such as anxiety and depression, which are expressed as an over-controlled and inner-directed pattern of development. However, increasingly, low-SES girls are at risk for externalizing problems such as aggression and antisocial behaviour.[40]

Low SES is linked to a number of factors that can further affect child development. Parents from low-income homes are more likely to experience depression (see chapter 4), be exposed to family violence (chapter 6), and have access to reduced levels of social support (chapter 8). These factors are in turn linked to unsupportive, inconsistent, and uninvolved parenting styles and poor parent–child attachment.[41] Social isolation and exclusion, which contribute to the incidence of socioemotional problems like anxiety, depression, and behavioural problems such as aggression and hyperactivity in children, are also associated with low SES.[42] Children reared in environments with "relational poverty," comprised of few social support network members, experience deprivation that negatively influences their cognitive neurodevelopment and behaviour.[43]

Nonetheless, by itself, SES is widely accepted to have a deleterious effect on the well-being and development of children and adolescents. Growing up in a home with low SES is linked not only to increased incidence of socio-emotional and behavioural problems, but also to cognitive and language delays, including reduced academic achievement.[44]

More recently, the impact of low SES has been observed in brain development. Researchers have charted structural differences in several areas of the brain among children from low-SES homes, including reduced grey matter volume in regions associated with school readiness and achievement, and delayed maturation of the frontal and temporal lobes — areas linked to planning and impulse control.[45]

While there does seem to be some association between how long a child spends in a low-SES home and the severity of its effects, a number of other factors also appear to be at play. Low SES may exert different influences on children's development at different stages in their lives (for example, early childhood versus adolescence), and the extent of its effects may be mitigated or exacerbated by a number of external factors, including the availability of resources to aid in parenting, level of social support, and parental mental health.[46] For example, low-SES parents of babies who have access to high quality child care or early intervention programs for their children such as Head Start have a better chance of promoting healthy development in their children. Also, older children who have attained some independence can seek out their own resources through school activities and clubs or their network of friends.

The exact cause of SES's impact on child development is subject to continuing debate. While some experts state that SES affects child development through the inability of parents to provide the material resources necessary for healthy child development,[47] others argue that it is the stress associated with low-SES households that affects children by interfering with parents' ability to engage in healthy serve and return interactions.[48,49] Still others offer a combination of these arguments, suggesting that parents in stressful economic situations are unable to provide the tangible (for example, money for outings, learning opportunities, and nutritious food) and intangible resources (serve and return interactions) necessary to support children's successful development.[50,51] In extreme cases, families of very low SES may not be able to provide the nutritious foods necessary for children's optimal body and brain development. It is likely the combination of both tangible and intangible resources that impact child development, which is reassuring, as parents who can marshal the energy for healthy serve and return interactions stand to support their children's success despite low SES.

SCORES ON THE SES QUESTIONS

Low Risk (Score: 6–10)

If you scored 6 or more, your SES is sufficient to support your child's development and is not likely reducing the quality of your parenting or serve and return interactions with your child.

> Mary gives a satisfied nod and closes the page. She has a score of 7, which puts her in the low-risk bracket. This fact has no impact on her day-to-day finances, but it comforts her all the same. Things are tight, but she supposes she's doing okay, all things considered. She still has a little cash socked away in her RRSP that she refuses to touch, and her Master's degree gives her some leverage if she loses her job or decides to look for something better.

Moderate Risk (Score: 3–5)

If you scored between 3 and 5, your SES may be affecting your child's development. You may find it difficult to make ends meet while also providing your child with books, day camps, educational trips, daycare, and other opportunities to enrich their early years. Financial difficulties may be causing stress in your life, which can in turn trickle down to your children. Often this occurs subtly, and even those parents who feel they are successfully keeping their children from the burden of these adult stresses are likely telegraphing their anxiety in unanticipated ways.

Seek opportunities for enrichment of your child's experiences that are low cost and can be accessed on a flexible schedule to accommodate long or atypical working hours. For children of any age, libraries offer many learning and enrichment opportunities, so sign up for a library card and use it. In addition to providing access to books and learning materials, many libraries have dedicated children's areas with crafts, toys, and educational activities, as well as a host of scheduled events tailored to children. For instance, the Toronto Public Library in Ontario runs regular song and story times for infants and toddlers as well as literacy and educational programs to assist school-age children in developing their reading skills. Also, libraries are often a local hub that link parents to other learning and enrichment opportunities in the community. Talk to your local librarian about accessing such programs for your child.

Other municipal services are worth investigating as well. Many urban centres offer educational and enrichment programs for children and families, often at little or no charge. For instance, in Ottawa, Ontario, parents have access to free playgroups in dozens of locations across the city. These programs, which run several times per week, are free of charge and expose children to various sensory-building activities, crafts, and games, and conclude with song and story time. Several outlets run toy libraries where parents can borrow developmentally appropriate toys free of charge. The city also runs free prenatal and postnatal clinics for new or expecting parents, which offer support and guidance on everything from breastfeeding to wellness checks.

It is also worth investigating municipal or provincial programs that subsidize low-income families. For instance, Ontario Works provides residents of the province with income support to help provide for basic needs, including health benefits and employment assistance through resume writing workshops, job counselling, and job-specific training. If searching for these programs online, try using search terms such as *low-income subsidy* or *poverty resources* and the name of your town/city/region. Many governments offer struggling families partial or complete fee reduction for daycare or day camp programs. Tracking down these opportunities can sometimes be challenging, but worth the effort. Community agencies such as the United Way and Home Start are available in Canada, Australia, the U.S., and the U.K. and can offer assistance in accessing resources. Your public health nurse or family physician can often provide helpful guidance in identifying and accessing local resources, too.

Mary bites her lip — 5 out of 10. Her results put her in the moderate-risk category, which means there's a chance Giovanni is being negatively affected by their financial situation. *The education part really stung me*, she reflects, once again wondering if she should go back to school and get her BA. Maybe then she could land a job with a bit more upward mobility. Of course, university isn't cheap, and would mean even more time away from Giovanni while she studied and completed coursework.

She scrolls down and checks some of the tips for individuals who scored in the moderate-risk bracket. She has a library card already, but it's been years since she went last. Maybe she should head down with Giovanni tomorrow and see if there are any children's programs available. If nothing else, she could read with him in the children's section for a while — something she'd always loved doing with her own parents as a child.

High Risk (Score: 0–2)

If you have scored in this category, there is a good chance that your child is being negatively affected by your SES. As suggested above in the Moderate Risk section, reach out to your public health nurse or family physician and ask for guidance in accessing subsides for child care, job training, educational opportunities, income support, and educational and recreational programs and services for your child. Many of these programs can be found online or on your regional or local government's website. Searching online or asking friends for advice about programs and services may be helpful, too. Also see above for ideas under the heading Moderate Risk.

If your child is younger than school age, seek out early intervention programs for low-SES children in your community such as Head Start or the Nurse–Family Partnership, available in many cities. These programs are designed to provide the enrichment that children need to thrive, despite their low SES. Early child development programs like these have been effective in promoting children's development,[52] with effects persisting into adolescence.[53] As suggested under the Moderate Risk section above, seeking opportunities for enrichment that cost little and can be accessed on a flexible schedule to accommodate long or atypical working hours are ideal.

If you require child care while you are working, and these programs are not available in your community, ensuring that your child's caregiving arrangement is of high quality is paramount. Questions you can ask your child's prospective caregiver or daycare include the following:

- Do you offer a curriculum for learning in the context of a caring, nurturing environment?
- Do you offer nutritious food and snacks?
- What is the ratio of children to caregivers?
- What is the education level of the caregivers?
- Do the caregivers understand the concept of serve and return interactions?
- Do the caregivers have the time and desire to engage in serve and return interactions with my child?
- What is the approach taken to infant/child crying?

With respect to childcare ratios, target three caregivers to ten children for infants younger than eighteen months; one caregiver to five children for toddlers up to thirty months; one caregiver to eight children for preschoolers up to six years; one caregiver to thirteen children for kindergartners up to sixty-eight months; one caregiver to fifteen children for primary and middle-school-age children up to thirteen years; and one caregiver to twenty children for older ages. Ideal childcare ratios will help. Ensure that your child has access to enough serve and return interactions with you and the other caregivers in his or her life (see chapter 2) to promote their development. Also ensure that your child's care providers have high-school education and at least some post-secondary training in early childhood development.

If your child is older, accessing free or subsidized recreational or educational programs in your community is also key. For instance, the Jumpstart program helps children from financially disadvantaged families from across Canada partake in sports and other physical activities at a reduced cost or for free. In Australia, the KidSport program provides subsidies for enrolment in sports teams and recreational classes. Many community municipalities, regional parks, churches, or other religious groups offer discounted activities, such as free summer day camps or youth leadership programs, for low-income children and youth. Military cadet programs are also a great free resource offering opportunities for youth to build social skills, self-discipline, and even musical ability (band training). School-based extra curricular programs offer similar advantages, so speak to your child's teacher about what is available. Offering children opportunities for learning and coaching from other caring adults in various settings can help children tremendously over the long term. If searching for these programs online, try using combinations of key terms such as *summer day camps, recreational programs, sports, leadership, band, youth, free, financial need, low-income* and the name of your town/city/region, or speak to your preferred health professional about finding programs in your community. If they do not have any suggestions, ask them if they know who might and be sure to follow up with who they recommend.

Finally, paying extra attention to your child's cues will likely help. As suggested above, it is unclear whether the lack of material resources puts children at risk or whether it is the stress associated with low SES that puts parenting and, in turn, children's development at risk. Finding ways to cope with and manage stress and any associated risks, such as mental health issues (see chapter 4) or family violence (see chapter 6) will likely be helpful. Focusing on improving serve and return interactions (chapter 2) and reflective function (chapter 7) may also help buffer the effects of low SES on your child's development.

> Mary feels her stomach drop a few inches. She scores a measly 2 out of 10, putting her firmly in the high-risk camp. She flicks back over the questions to see if she'd made a mistake somewhere. She finds no errors. Are things really that bad? She thinks on Giovanni's recent behaviour, the way he sometimes acts out to get her attention, which she has to admit can be hard to take. She's just so tired at the end of the day and the

nights offer no real relief. It seems that when she's not working to earn money she's worrying about how little she has. The two activities have merged into an unbreakable wall of anxiety over which it can be all but impossible to climb.

She calls her family doctor and makes an appointment for the next day. The website where she'd completed the questionnaire suggests speaking with a health professional about programs available in her area, and her doctor is a trustworthy and compassionate person.

Chapter 4

Depression

Depression is the thief that steals
motherhood.

— Cheryl Beck

Josalinde stirs her tea. The spoon rattles against the mug,
a bright tinkling sound muffled by the cup's liquid contents. She gulps it only to find the tea has gone cold.
How long has she been stirring? With a sigh, she dumps
the tea into the sink, flicks on the kettle, and collapses
back into the kitchen chair, exhausted by her efforts.

She rubs her eyes but the gritty feeling behind her
eyelids won't go away. She doesn't understand how
she can be so tired all the time. It's been two months
since she returned to Vancouver from her time over-
seas and yet she still feels plagued with jetlag.

From down the hall, Josalinde's ears catch Maxine's tentative whimpers as she wakes from her afternoon nap. It strikes Josalinde as an ugly, ominous sound. Her belly lurches, upset by either the cold tea or her guilt, she's not sure. She should be happy to hear her daughter waking up, eager to rejoin her after the short separation mandated by her slumber. Instead she fumes and checks her watch — 1:15 p.m. It was a short one. They're always short ones.

Maxine's crying gets louder, an endless crescendo that never seems to break. Biting the inside of her cheek, Josalinde fishes out her phone from her purse, finds her mom's number among her frequent contacts, and hits call. Her mother answers on the fifth ring.

"Yes, Jo, what is it?"

"Hi, Mom," says Josalinde. "What do you have on the go today?"

"Quite a bit at the moment. The girls from Project Share are coming by to plan our fundraiser, and I've got a shift this afternoon."

"Oh." Josalinde draws meaningless pictures in the ring of moisture her tea mug left on the kitchen table. "I guess that's pretty set, huh?"

"I'd say so. Why?"

"I was just wondering if you could watch Maxine for a bit."

Josalinde had always expected such requests to elicit coos of joy in a new grandmother. Instead she met a moment's stony silence, followed by the stern cluck of her mother's tongue. "No, I don't think that'll be possible today."

"I see."

"What is it you need a sitter for anyhow? It's not as if you're working."

A sharp response rises to the tip of Josalinde's tongue. She sheaths it, leading with something softer instead. "I'm just not feeling very well. I think I might be coming down with something. I don't want Maxine to catch a flu."

"Well surely Peter can help out."

"He's away, Mom. For work."

"Yes, of course he is. Always travelling, isn't he?"

"He has an important job," Josalinde says. She feels prickly at her mother's insinuation, but in her heart she agrees. He really is always travelling, much more than you'd think a middle manager of a regional company would. Josalinde had started to suspect that he'd volunteered for more away duties as a reprieve from her and Maxine. Or that some of those trips weren't really for business at all.

"Yes. Well, do call if it becomes truly urgent," says Josalinde's mom, in a voice suggesting that such claims of urgency would be taken at her discretion.

"Right. Thanks." Josalinde irritably slams the phone down. Maxine's crying has risen to a steady howl. With rising agitation, Josalinde combs her mind for a friend she can call upon to talk to or give her a hand. She can't think of a single person. All the people she'd known had either moved away while she was gone or developed a strange distance at her return. As if she were not the person they remembered but a pale and offsetting facsimile. Grimacing, irritated, she forces herself to rise.

The stairway stretching from the living room to the bedroom hall seems to stretch on forever, each step like a flight of its own. After an eternity she reaches Maxine's room, holds her breath, her body a-quiver, and enters.

No longer blunted by the bedroom door, Maxine's crying reaches a new and sharper pitch. Josalinde picks her up and holds her woodenly in her arms. She pats her back, the gesture clumsy, but Maxine cries less, though still whimpering. After a few minutes of unsuccessful consoling she digs her phone out from her pocket and dials another of her frequent contacts. A girl's voice answers, blinding with impossible cheeriness.

"Hello, Karen speaking."

"Hi, Karen. It's Josalinde."

"Oh hey, Mrs. Reed. What's up?"

With a cringe of exertion and irriation, Josalinde changes her monotone to something resembling casual speech. "Oh nothing, really. I was just wondering if you'd be interested in watching Maxine for me. I'm feeling a little under the weather and could use a breather."

"Yeah, sure. When were you thinking?"

"Whenever works for you."

"Would three o'clock be okay?"

Josalinde checks her watch. It's now 1:24 p.m. "I was thinking more like two."

"Yeah, I think I could swing that. See you then."

"Right. Bye."

Josalinde pulls up her shirt and lets Maxine latch. The whimpering ceases in an instant, replaced by the gentler but still unpleasant sound of sucking. There was a time when Josalinde found breastfeeding a joyous, bonding experience, but recently and especially today, the sucking and heavy breathing of her little one just made her skin crawl.

When Karen arrives — knowing enough by now to let herself in — Josalinde hands the now fed and dozing Maxine off with a small nod of appreciation.

She can't wait to crawl into bed to sleep. But a combination of fatigue and heightened agitation refuses to let go of her addled mind. From the mire of her blankets, never sleeping, Josalinde finally admits to herself that something is wrong. She forces herself from the confusion long enough to grab her phone and search online for resources — anything that might explain what she's feeling. She finds a questionnaire, which asks about how she has been feeling over the last week.

THE DEPRESSION SYMPTOMS SURVEY

The following survey is frequently used in research and clinical practice to assess parents' level of depressive symptoms. Take the survey now and then see the end of the chapter for your results and recommended resources.

The Depression Symptoms Survey

How often did you experience the following in the last week?

1. I was bothered by things that usually don't bother me.

	Rarely or never (>1 day)	Some or a little of the time (1–2 days)	Occasionally or a moderate amount of time (3–4 days)	Most or all of the time (5–7 days)
SCORE	0	1	2	3

2. I had trouble keeping my mind on what I was doing.

	Rarely or never (>1 day)	Some or a little of the time (1–2 days)	Occasionally or a moderate amount of time (3–4 days)	Most or all of the time (5–7 days)
SCORE	0	1	2	3

3. I felt depressed.

	Rarely or never (>1 day)	Some or a little of the time (1–2 days)	Occasionally or a moderate amount of time (3–4 days)	Most or all of the time (5–7 days)
SCORE	0	1	2	3

4. I felt that everything I did was an effort.

	Rarely or never (>1 day)	Some or a little of the time (1–2 days)	Occasionally or a moderate amount of time (3–4 days)	Most or all of the time (5–7 days)
SCORE	0	1	2	3

5. I felt hopeful about the future.

	Rarely or never (>1 day)	Some or a little of the time (1–2 days)	Occasionally or a moderate amount of time (3–4 days)	Most or all of the time (5–7 days)
SCORE	3	2	1	0

6. I felt fearful.

Rarely or never (>1 day)	Some or a little of the time (1–2 days)	Occasionally or a moderate amount of time (3–4 days)	Most or all of the time (5–7 days)
SCORE			
0	1	2	3

7. My sleep was restless.

Rarely or never (>1 day)	Some or a little of the time (1–2 days)	Occasionally or a moderate amount of time (3–4 days)	Most or all of the time (5–7 days)
SCORE			
0	1	2	3

8. I was happy.

Rarely or never (>1 day)	Some or a little of the time (1–2 days)	Occasionally or a moderate amount of time (3–4 days)	Most or all of the time (5–7 days)
SCORE			
3	2	1	0

9. I felt lonely.

Rarely or never (>1 day)	Some or a little of the time (1–2 days)	Occasionally or a moderate amount of time (3–4 days)	Most or all of the time (5–7 days)
SCORE			
0	1	2	3

10. I felt I could not get going.

Rarely or never (>1 day)	Some or a little of the time (1–2 days)	Occasionally or a moderate amount of time (3–4 days)	Most or all of the time (5–7 days)
SCORE			
0	1	2	3

Tally responses in each row:

Score 7 or less: read *low risk*

Score 8–9: read *moderate risk*

Score 10+: read *high risk*

ALL ABOUT DEPRESSION

When discussing depression, health care professionals use a more technical term: major depressive disorder, or MDD for short. MDD is one of the most commonly diagnosed disorders among adults, affecting about seven percent of all adults in the U.S. in 2015.[54] The symptoms of depression tend to last around three or four months before abating but often resurface. About sixty percent of people who experience a depressive episode will go on to suffer a second episode. Seventy percent of these individuals will suffer a third episode, and ninety percent of those who experience three episodes will continue to experience them down the road.[55]

Adults with MDD may experience a range of symptoms, including feelings of sadness or emptiness, diminished pleasure in activities they once enjoyed, fatigue or loss of energy, and excessive feelings of worthlessness or guilt. Not surprisingly, these symptoms often negatively affect work success and relationships with children, partners, family, and friends. Symptoms must be experienced consistently during a two-week period and represent a change from previous functioning to be considered a MDD.

WHAT CAUSES DEPRESSION?

As we learned in chapter 1, trauma, stress, and family history can all contribute to depression. Biological explanations for depression have been proposed, with alterations in the stress response system (known in technical terms as the hypothalamic-pituitary-adrenal axis), inflammation (which may be linked to early life stress and trauma), and genetic vulnerabilities ranking as the most likely culprits.[56] Lack of exercise over a prolonged period has also been seen as an exacerbating factor.[57] While depression can strike anyone, mothers and fathers appear more susceptible to different triggers. For mothers, likely factors include a lack of social support, isolation from friends and family, low self-esteem, and feelings of incompetence.[58] Single mothers lacking support may be particularly at risk. For fathers, depression can stem from the social expectations associated with fatherhood, such as the traditional role of the man as the family's provider.[59] This sense of newfound responsibility can trigger depressive symptoms.[60] Marital dissatisfaction is another strong risk factor for both mothers[61] and fathers.[62]

POSTPARTUM DEPRESSION IMPACTS MOTHERS AND FATHERS

Postpartum depression (PPD), is a type of MDD which happens after the birth of a baby. It is different from, but often confused with, postpartum blues or postpartum psychosis, which represent its more mild and severe relatives, respectively. The postpartum blues (or "baby blues") usually occur in the first two weeks following the child's birth and are characterized by sadness lasting a day or two. About fifty to eighty percent of women will experience the baby blues, almost all of whom will recover without the development of any additional symptoms.[63] On the other end of the spectrum, postpartum psychosis involves severe breaks from reality and, in worst cases, can result in harm to the baby, the mother, or others. While postpartum psychosis is a serious condition that requires medical intervention, it is also quite rare, occurring in roughly 0.001 percent of new mothers.[64] Nearly fifty percent of mothers with PPD experience intrusive thoughts about hurting themselves or their baby, but only when this thinking develops into a plan or is accompanied by extreme confusion does it become characteristic of psychosis.[65] The blues are not believed to affect parenting, and while psychosis is a very serious condition that can affect parenting, these mothers require specialized medical help. Thus, only MDD and PPD will be discussed here.

Postpartum depression is most commonly thought of as affecting women, but it can also affect men, either directly by experiencing depression themselves during the postpartum period or indirectly through their experiences supporting and coping with their partner's symptoms.[66] About fifteen percent of new mothers will develop PPD symptoms.[67] Mothers are more likely to develop PPD in the first twelve weeks postpartum,[68] but most health professionals will consider any depression in the first year after baby's birth to be PPD. A lot of women relapse, with one study of over ten thousand Canadian families showing that sixty-three percent of women who experience symptoms of depression after their baby's birth will have their symptoms return at least once over the next eleven to twelve years.[69] Fathers have been less studied, but we know that among men whose partners experience PPD, a quarter to one-half will also experience depression.[70] A study that examined nearly thirty thousand fathers found that approximately ten percent will experience depression in the first year postpartum. Unlike mothers, whose PPD symptoms usually begin soon after the birth of their baby, depression in fathers begins later and more gradually, often following the onset in their partners.[71]

Postpartum depression places mothers at increased risk of social isolation due to lack of energy, fatigue, and feelings of incompetence, worthlessness, and helplessness. Mothers are more likely to rely on their partners for support,[72] which can cause strain on the relationship, leading to disagreements, hostility, and even withdrawal of social support.[73]

Fathers suffering from depression alongside their partners have also reported marital difficulties associated with poor communication and feelings of being overwhelmed, isolated, stigmatized, and frustrated.[74] Whether depressed themselves or coping with their partner's depression, the new father's stress is magnified by attempts to cope with the demands of his partner's depression and the new infant in the family on top of any previous commitments he may have (for example, older children, work).[75] There is even evidence of intergenerational effects of depression on couples. In a study of marital couples, partners who were raised by a depressed mother or father felt sad and angry as adults and experienced their partners as hostile, competitive, mistrusting, detached, less agreeable, and less nurturing than couples who had not had a depressed parent.[76] Depression can even increase the risk for domestic violence between mothers and fathers,[77] and the risk for separation and divorce.[78]

RELATIONSHIPS WITH CHILDREN AFFECTED BY SYMPTOMS OF DEPRESSION

Depression is considered by the Harvard Center on the Developing Child as a "toxic" stressor affecting children's development because it interferes with a parent's ability to be sensitive and responsive to his or her children, which in turn affects child development. Sensitivity and responsiveness between parents and children are also referred to as a "serve and return" relationship, which we address in greater detail in chapter 2. Sensitivity refers to a parent's ability to observe baby's cues (or "serves," in the same sense as serving a tennis ball) and identify what need the baby is signalling. Responsiveness entails the parent's ability to answer the cue in an appropriate way (to return the serve, in the way that a good tennis player will swat back their partner's serve). This two-way exchange of cues and replies are the foundation on which babies develop secure attachment with their parents — and that is a very good thing, as secure attachment is linked to a host of positive outcomes that parents want for their children: healthy social and emotional adjustment,[79] better cognitive development,[80] superior brain development,[81] and overall improved health.

Depressed parents can miss serve and return opportunities, or even reduce the overall quality of their relationship with their baby or child in a variety of ways:

- failing to provide positive feedback
- speaking less often and more slowly with their children
- being less affectionate
- showing less firm or consistent discipline
- offering criticism, hostility, and rejection towards children
- perceiving normal child behaviour in a negative light (for example, interpreting fussiness from hunger or boredom as being "bratty")[82]

As a result of these behaviours, children of parents with PPD are at an increased risk for a number of developmental delays and health problems. For example, compared to children of mothers who were not depressed, children of mothers who are depressed are more likely to

- be difficult, fussy, whiny, or protesting[83]
- be asthmatic[84]
- have decreased vocabularies[85]
- have behavioural problems, such as aggression or hyperactivity[86]
- have decreased intellectual and motor development.[87,88]

Fathers' depression also has a negative impact on the quality of their serve and return relationships. Compared to fathers who are not suffering from depression, depressed fathers demonstrate less warmth toward their children, tend to be more controlling,[89] and are significantly less engaged in reading and other kinds of literacy-building activities.[90] While most research on postpartum depression's effects have focused on mothers, studies have linked paternal PPD with an increased risk of behavioural problems in children, such as anger, aggression, and hyperactivity.[91] Boys in particular may be more susceptible to the negative consequences of PPD, exhibiting more antisocial, active, aggressive, hyper-active, and distractible behaviours,[92] as well as below-average vocabulary and IQ when compared to their peers whose parents do not suffer from PPD.[93] Notably, boys exposed to both maternal depression and marital conflict during the postpartum period are more likely to display behavioural problems like hyperactivity and increased aggression.

It is important to note that the risk for child adjust-ment problems, such as behavioural acting out, associated with depressive symptoms in mothers seems comparable to that of exposure to depressive symptoms in fathers.[94] However, what is most concerning about *mothers'* depres-sion is that children's behavioural problems *seem to persist, even when the depressive symptoms have gone away.*[95] This has been attributed to the quality of the serve and return relationship established between mothers and children during the depressive episode, which continues after the mother has recovered.[96] While this is alarming, it also gives health professionals a big hint about where they must focus their work to help families affected by depression in mothers or both parents. In fact, my own research has shown that among mothers with depression, when we examined factors that impacted the stress-hormone (cortisol) levels of their babies (recall from the Introduction how cortisol can be neurotoxic at sustained high levels), it was not how depressed mothers were, but rather the quality of their serve and return relationship that most reduced the cortisol levels. In other words, the toxic stressor of postpartum depression was made tolerable by the quality of the serve and return relationships that mothers established with their children.

SCORES ON THE DEPRESSION SYMPTOMS SURVEY

Low Risk (Score: 0–7)

You are at low risk for depression.

> Josalinde checks the tally at the end of the questionnaire. She has scored a 3, signalling low risk. The number gives her some comfort, as the questions helped her reflect on the many ways she could feel worse. Things have been hard, and between the culture shock of her return to Canada and exhaustion over Maxine's care, it's no wonder she feels tired and agitated sometimes. Eventually things will get better. Comforted by this thought, she finally drifts off to sleep.

Moderate Risk (Score: 8–9)

This score suggests that you have some symptoms that put you at risk for developing depression. There are things you can do to minimize the possibility that this will turn into a full-blown PPD or MDD. As with many of the conditions discussed in this book, relationships are key. Think about the network around you, be they your partner, family, or close friends. Do they provide a positive environment? Can you count on them when things are difficult? Establishing a social safety net will help buffer you from the stressors that can bring on or exacerbate depression. Research has also found that regular exercise provides a safeguard against depression. Refer to Chapter 8: Social Support and Co-Parenting for more information and tips.

Josalinde scores an 8. She casts her mind back over the past weeks, recalls the moments of listlessness and fatigue scattered like jagged stones over her path. She feels like she's stumbled a lot lately, though she isn't entirely without a shoulder to lean on. Her mother helps when she can and while she might grumble, Josalinde knows she can count on her in a pinch. And Peter is an attentive father when he's home, though she knows he works hard and the evenings can be tough on him, too.

Scrolling to the top of her phone's browser, she types in *support for mothers with depression in Toronto* and scans the top hits. There are more programs out there than she'd expected, from private counselling to informal chats at a nearby coffee shop. Midway down the list, she spies an ad for a moms-only exercise group at a local gym. She clicks the link and after a few minutes browsing the details signs herself up. She's been feeling out of shape lately, and it'll be good to meet some other new moms. Luckily she has Karen, who's happy to babysit anytime. Rested and finally relaxed, Josalinde rises and smiles at the sound of Maxine in the other room.

High Risk (Score: 10 or More)

I am so glad you have found this book if it has helped you determine that you have depression. MDD and PPD are serious conditions that require treatment. Fortunately, there are a number of treatment methods available that have proven effective in many cases. Some examples include the following:

- psychotherapy, including interpersonal or cognitive behavioural therapy[97]
- psychological counselling or support
- peer–professional support systems like peer support groups[98]
- medications such as selective serotonin reuptake inhibitors (for example, Prozac)[99]

Along with these approaches, exercise, improved sleep, and even micronutrient supplementation in the form of multivitamins may be helpful. There is a growing body of research that supports the use of micronutrient supplementation. Contact True Hope (www.truehope.com) or Hardy Nutritionals (www.hardynutritionals.com) for more information. Patients can respond in contrasting ways to treatments, so keep trying until you find one that works for you. It is vital, however, that you address your symptoms.

One recommended approach for helping mothers deal with symptoms of depression follows this order:

1. Mothers enter treatment, which may involve medication, psychotherapy, or counselling, and focus on improving sleep, nutrition, social support, and reducing disturbing and intrusive thoughts.

2. Gradually, as symptoms improve, the focus of treatment changes from symptoms to focusing on improving nurturing relationships with babies and children, characterized by healthy serve and return interaction.

3. Finally, after mother's symptoms and the maternal–infant/child relationship are stabilized, the father is involved in therapeutic work on any problems that remain, such as the marital relationship or the father's own struggles.[100]

However, given the bi-directional relationship between marital dysfunction and parental depression, quality of marital relationships may be an area to explore beforehand. I urge you to consider your unique situation and advocate for the order of therapy that you think would work best.

Taking care of yourself and your relationships, especially those between you and your children and you and your partner, is essential. Depression can reduce intimacy and connectedness between partners, which can further negatively impact symptoms. Conversely, a supportive partner can increase the effectiveness of treatments, help prevent relapse, be a role model or stable presence, and act as an important buffer for children while their mothers' serve and return relationships are impeded. Given this host of benefits, fathers should play a key role in helping mothers through their PPD.

As invaluable as a father's support might be, it is worth noting that it, too, is subject to external factors. Fathers may be suffering from depression themselves, afflicted with another illness or condition, overwhelmed by stressors, or in marital distress. Any number of factors can impede a father's ability to support his partner. Men, however, are statistically less likely to seek care for themselves, so families must ensure that fathers themselves get the vital support they need.

Some depressed parents may be parenting alone. If this describes your situation, identifying sources of co-parenting support (see chapter 8 for ideas) and protecting your serve and return relationship with your child is essential (see chapter 2). In addition to seeking help for your depressive symptoms, identifying and attaining support resources (for example, family, friends) for you and your child can buffer your child from the effects of depression while you are returning to wellness. Until you are well, focusing also on maintaining and strengthening the quality of your serve and return interactions with your child can promote your child's resiliency in the long run. Remember that research shows it is not the depressive symptoms per se that predict the problems in children's development, but rather how the depressive symptoms undermine the serve and return relationship between parents and children.

Finally, if you are parenting a baby, interventions focused on enhancing serve and return have been found to improve relationships between parents and babies; more intense interventions may also improve health and developmental outcomes for children. Due to the rapid brain growth occurring during babyhood, ensuring high quality serve and return relationships is critical for optimizing babies' brain architecture; that said, serve and return is also important with older children. Trying to preserve the quality of your relationship with your child at any age is necessary as you take steps to treat and manage your depression. Chapter 2 offers suggestions on how to improve your serve and return relationship with your baby or child. Chapter 7, which discusses reflective function, may also be helpful in promoting the sensitivity needed for healthy serve and return relationships.

If searching online for resources in your community, try using the search terms *postpartum depression, depression support groups,* or *mental health help line* and the name of your town/city/region. Many online resources can be found using the same terms. A few I recommend include

- Postpartum Support International (www.postpartum.net)

- The Marcé Society for Perinatal Mental Health (https://marcesociety.com)
- National Alliance on Mental Illness (www.nami.org/Find-Support/NAMI-HelpLine)

Many books are available on mental health issues and parents as well. Try *Postpartum Depression and Anxiety: A Self-Help Guide for Mothers* by the Pacific Post Partum Support Society; *This Isn't What I Expected: Overcoming Postpartum Depression* by Karen Kleiman and Valerie Raskin; or *Parenting Well When You're Depressed: A Complete Resource for Maintaining a Healthy Family* by Henry Nicholson.

Josalinde stares at the screen, where her score is displayed in stark black numerals: 15. Looking at it brings on a pang of fear but also a slight measure of relief. The events of the last few months, many of them seemingly disparate and random, suddenly shift into alignment.

She recalls all those moments of loneliness, the waves of exhaustion that crashed over her whenever she tried to get groceries or do the dishes, the sudden flares of anger and irritation at Peter or Maxine over the mildest infractions.

And then there were the thoughts. Those ugly, horrible thoughts when Maxine is screaming in her arms and nothing she does can stop it and she just wants to throw her to the ground and walk away. She would never do such a thing, would sooner cut off her own head than harm her child, yet the scary thoughts always seem to squeeze in through the cracks.

She takes out her phone and dials her doctor's office. The receptionist answers on the second ring.

"Hello, Main Street Medical Clinic. How can I help you?"

"Hi there," Josalinde says. "This is Josalinde Reed. I need to make an appointment, as soon as possible."

The receptionist asks, "What is the reason for the appointment?"

Josalinde pauses, biting her lip for moment. She answers, "I think I have postpartum depression and I want to find out what I can do to get better."

The receptionist says, "Okay, it's good you called about that. The doctor has an opening tomorrow at 2:00 p.m. Does that work for you?"

Chapter 5
Addictions

When I was on drugs, there was a monstrous side to me, but I'm not really like that.

— Elton John

The noise fills John's ears. It reverberates throughout the room, an incessant pounding that seems to come from everywhere and nowhere. Is there someone at the door? Does the washing machine have an unbalanced load? Are the kids throwing bouncy balls around again?

As he reaches for his glasses on the nightstand, intent on solving the mystery, John realizes that the sound is the pounding of blood in his temples. His head is suffused with relentless throbbing pain and starts to spin like a cacophonous merry-go-round. In the pounding haze, he knocks his glasses to the floor and the sharp sound sends shards of pain, bright and red and horrible, through his head. He cries out and is jarred by yet another sensation — his throat is so dry, it's like he's swallowed sand paper.

Water, he thinks, the plea so intense it's almost audible. *I need water.* He gingerly slides out of bed, locates his glasses, and slouches to the bathroom like something wretched and suffering, a wounded animal with fading strength.

He thrusts his head into the sink basin and turns the tap on full blast. His mouth opens feebly at the torrent of cold water. He paws open the medicine cabinet and grabs the Tylenol, scattering and overturning a half dozen other bottles in the process. *I'll pick that up later*, he thinks. Moving with the efficiency of extensive practise, he presses the heel of his hand against the lid, twists it free, and taps out two pills into his palm. After a moment's contemplation he adds a third, tosses them into his mouth, and washes them down with another gulp from the tap.

The water and pills start to do their work, and he's able to think beyond the fog of pain engulfing him and recall its cause. They'd had a late meeting at work yesterday to discuss an upcoming whitepaper. Someone had proposed grabbing a bite afterwards, and some other damn fool — it was probably him — had suggested capping the night off with a pint at O'Malley's. The pint in question grew with its usual malignancy to a pitcher or so, metastasizing into straight whiskey after the lightweights had gone home. He'd continued well into the morning and got home … somehow. A glance out the window reveals an empty driveway. So he'd cabbed it, at least. The car was probably still at the office. Thank God for small favours.

He showers and shaves and leaves the bathroom feeling like something approaching human. He checks his watch. Quarter past seven. Quickening his pace, he raps his knuckles on the boys' bedroom door.

"Up and at 'em, kids. We'll have to hustle this morning." He listens for signs of life beyond the door and hears instead the industrious sounds of kitchen prep work: cupboards closing, cereal pouring, the toaster dinging. Good old Sandy. Eleven years old and he's already taking charge, getting himself and Bo off to school without any prodding.

His paternal pride soon sours into guilt. *You shouldn't have gone out at all*, mutters a stern voice in his head — his ex-wife Stacey's, he realizes vaguely. *You know it's never just one pint.*

I had no choice, he sulks. *I'm a regional manager. I can't just pack it in when the boys are heading out. What's that gonna do to morale?*

The other voice does not dignify this excuse with a reply.

He enters the kitchen and finds his two boys sitting at the table eating bowls of cereal. Sandy ignores his entrance, but Bo looks up and shoots him a toothy smile flecked with bits of food.

"Hey, Dad!"

"Morning, Bo. Morning, Sandy. How'd you sleep?"

Sandy glances up for a moment, says nothing, and resumes stirring his cereal. Bo, oblivious to his brother's slight, answers cheerfully.

"Good! Today we're gonna watch a movie about dinosaurs! I've never seen it before but Marlon has and he says it's really good!"

"Uh huh. Wow." John fixes himself a coffee while Bo prattles on. He tries to listen but the words feel harsh on his ears. He adds the odd non-committal interjection and focuses his main attention on the coffee. As the brew percolates he takes his biggest mug out of the cupboard, wincing as it clatters against the other cups. He pours the still-boiling coffee into the mug and takes a sip, sighing with pleasure despite the pain of the hot liquid on his lips.

"Dad," says Bo, his sunny tone clouding over. "Dad, you're not listening."

"Sure I am. Dinosaurs. Great."

"I wasn't talking about dinosaurs anymore. I was asking if I could go to Jordan's after school."

"What? Yeah, fine." John rubs his forehead. His son's whining pierced his frontal lobe like a corkscrew.

His cereal done, Sandy clears the table and gets Bo his backpack. John smiles as Sandy helps his younger brother with his shoelaces.

"Thanks for helping out, Sandy," John says.

Sandy looks at him, unsmiling. "Someone has to." He ties his own shoes and leaves for the bus without another word. Bo follows him, pausing at the threshold.

"Dad, are you mad at us or something?"

"What? No, no. I'm just tired is all. I'll make it up to you this evening. We can all do something fun together."

"I thought you said I could go to Jordan's."

"Hmm? Oh, right. Another time then. Don't miss your bus."

After downing his coffee, John taps his phone and orders a taxi. He puts the mug in the sink and waits at the living room window for his ride. While he waits, he takes out his phone again, types *Do I have a drinking problem?* into his search bar, and presses enter. The first link takes him to a questionnaire on drug and alcohol addiction.

ALCOHOL AND DRUG USE SURVEY

The following survey is an adapted version of a screening tool routinely used to assess adults for alcohol dependence. I have adapted it to include other addictions as well. Take the survey now and then see the end of the chapter for your results and recommended resources.

Alcohol and Drug Use Survey

1. Do you feel you drink/use drugs more than most people?

Yes _____ No _____

2. Have you ever awakened the morning after drinking/using drugs the night before and found that you could not remember a part of the evening?

Yes _____ No _____

---

3. Does any near relative or close friend ever worry or complain about your drinking/drug use?

Yes _____ No _____

4. Do you find it difficult to stop your drinking/drug use after taking a small amount (for example, one or two drinks, one hit)?

Yes _____ No _____

5. Do you ever feel bad about your drinking/drug use?

Yes _____ No _____

6. Have you ever attended a meeting of Alcoholics Anonymous (AA) or Narcotics Anonymous?

Yes _____ No _____

7. Have you ever gotten into physical fights when drinking/using drugs?

Yes _____ No _____

8. Has drinking/drug use ever created problems between you and a near relative or close friend?

Yes _____ No _____

9. Has any family member or close friend gone to anyone for help about your drinking/drug use?

Yes _____ No _____

10. Have you ever lost friends because of your drinking/drug use?

Yes _____ No _____

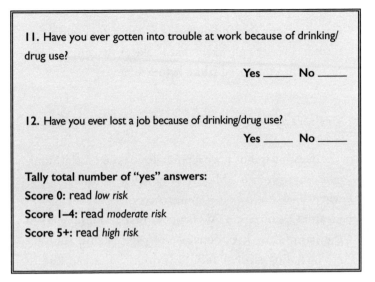

11. Have you ever gotten into trouble at work because of drinking/drug use?

Yes _____ No _____

12. Have you ever lost a job because of drinking/drug use?

Yes _____ No _____

Tally total number of "yes" answers:
Score 0: read *low risk*
Score 1–4: read *moderate risk*
Score 5+: read *high risk*

ALCOHOL AND DRUG USE AROUND THE WORLD

In Western society, alcohol has taken a central role in many adult social functions. Just imagine watching a football game without a cold one to wash down the hotdog and popcorn, foregoing that glass of Malbec at the office wine and cheese, or sipping a Diet Coke instead of a frothy beer après-ski. For a lot of us, it is almost unthinkable.

Throughout North and South America, Europe, Australia, Africa, and large parts of Asia — most of the world, in short — consuming moderate amounts of alcohol is simply part of adulthood for most people. And given the movement towards legalizing cannabis in some parts of the world — with legislation passing or tabled in

Canada, Germany, and several U.S. states, for example —
it seems increasingly likely that a toke or two might wend
its way into the social fabric before long.

Use and Abuse

The question is thus at what point does regular social indul-
gence morph into addictive or destructive behaviour —
when does use become abuse? According to the World
Health Organization (WHO), "substance abuse refers to
the harmful or hazardous use of psychoactive substances including alcohol and illicit drugs." This can lead to
addiction, characterized by changes in behaviour, thinking, and even the function of body systems. These behaviours cause people to keep drinking alcohol in spite of
the well-known negative health effects, which in large
doses can increase the risk of cancer, liver cirrhosis, diabetes, and cardiovascular disease.

Addicted people have a strong desire to consume
their substance of choice — be it alcohol or any other
drug — and have difficulty controlling their intake, even
when their consumption begins eating away at the rest of
their lives. The addiction overshadows everything, taking
more and more from the addict until there is nothing left
for them to give. While some substances (for example,
tobacco, opioids) have chemically addictive properties,
addiction is at its core a psychological illness. An addict
can be addicted to anything, from cocaine to food to
shopping. However, addictions to alcohol and narcotic

drugs seem to cause the most suffering in relationships between parents and children.*

How Big Is the Problem?

The WHO recognizes that worldwide, sixteen percent of adults consume too much alcohol. Statistics from the United States released in 2015 show that fifty percent of adults age twenty-six or older report having used illicit drugs in their lifetime, and eight percent have used in the last month. Among illicit drugs, cannabis was most common, with forty-six percent of respondents reporting lifetime use and about seven percent reporting use in the last month. Statistics are similar in the United Kingdom, with eight percent of adults reporting the use of an illicit drug in the last year. In general, women require less of a substance than men to become addicted. Women and men also appear to have different reasons for abusing drugs and alcohol, with women more likely than men to report factors such as controlling their weight, helping with fatigue, and treating mental health problems as drivers for use. Unfortunately, women who abuse drugs and alcohol are more likely to have mental health problems such as depression (see chapter 4). Women also report using drugs and alcohol to help cope with domestic violence (see chapter 7).

---

* While tobacco addiction is another unhealthy substance that poses threats to children in terms of cancer and respiratory risks, among others, it does not carry the same risk to relationships as the more reality-altering psychoactive substances of alcohol and illicit drugs, including cannabis. As well, there are other purported addictions, such as to shopping or sugar, but these addictions generally do not carry heightened risk to interaction quality in relationships, which can affect children's development, and so are not the focus here.

HOW DOES PARENTAL ADDICTION AFFECT CHILDREN?

Not surprisingly, the time, energy, and money an addiction draws from affected parents leaves little left over for children, who often face neglect as a result. You may remember that one of the questions in the ACE (Adverse Childhood Experiences) questionnaire in chapter 1 is about problem drinking or drug use in parents. Sadly, nearly thirty percent of American adults report that they grew up with someone in their household who was a problem drinker or who used illicit drugs. Both the Harvard Center on the Developing Child and the Centers for Disease Control and Prevention consider parental addiction "toxic" to children's health and development, ranking it alongside parental depression and family violence.

As early as 1977, researchers identified a number of conditions that appeared with noticeable frequency among children exposed to alcohol during pregnancy, including unique facial characteristics, cognitive challenges, and behavioural problems. These disparate conditions were ultimately found to have a common root, which became known as Fetal Alcohol Spectrum Disorder (FASD). Today, most doctors and scientists agree that any amount of alcohol in pregnancy is too risky for the developing fetus. Other illicit substances like crack cocaine are also extremely hazardous to fetal and, ultimately, child development.

In recent years, the risks associated with drug use during pregnancy have filtered into the public consciousness, making the consumption of alcohol or other drugs among pregnant mothers taboo. Educational campaigns in the form of ads and public service announcements have been widespread. Many pregnant mothers even give up caffeine for the duration of their pregnancies, for fear it might cause unknown damage to their developing child's nervous system.

The WHO reports that the effects of alcohol on children and families can include the following:

- injuries, intentional or otherwise (for example, accidents)
- neglect or abuse
- defaulting on social role in families (for example, failing to establish and maintain healthy serve and return relationships)
- damage to personal possessions (for example, destroying child's favourite toy)
- fear, anxiety, and worry
- loss of peace of mind (for example, concern over drinker's actions)

Not surprisingly, these observations extend to children and families of other types of addicts, too. When both parents are addicted, the risk of all types of poor outcomes increases, especially physical and sexual abuse.[101] In general, children of substance abusers are at greater risk for abusive and neglectful parenting.

Many of the outcomes observed in children of addicts overlap with the outcomes observed in children from other risky environments, such as those affected by physical abuse or parental depression.[102] Children whose parents suffer from addiction are more likely to develop a number of mental disorders, including becoming addicts themselves as adolescents. Specifically, children exposed to parental substance abuse are at increased risk for cognitive deficits, language delays, emotional problems, and behavioural disorders.[103] They commonly live in homes with high levels of stress, poor communication, excessive permissiveness, neglect, and violence. And because parents are in denial or fearful of reaching out for help due to stigma, these children often suffer in silence, unidentified and unassisted.

The negative effects of growing up with parents suffering from addiction often extend into adulthood, with adults raised in such families more likely to be depressed, abuse substances themselves, have self-esteem issues,[104] and struggle with managing stress. They also have reduced well-being, achievement,[105] and more negative marital relationships. For example, one study showed that as married adult children of alcoholics, wives are more likely to report lower marital intimacy, and men are more likely to feel less satisfied in the marriage and to be more physically aggressive, especially if their mother was the alcoholic. Children raised in alcoholic families often carry the problematic effects of their early family environment into their adult romantic relationships.[106]

HOW DOES ADDICTION INFLUENCE PARENTING? REDUCING SERVE AND RETURN

Every parent knows that parenting requires energy, investment, and near-constant attention, which can take its toll on the healthiest of individuals. But for addicts, the burden of parenthood is extreme. Parenting stress among a sample of addicted mothers was at the ninetieth percentile, which means these mothers had higher stress than ninety percent of the normal parent population.[107] Substance-abusing mothers are also at increased risk of low self-esteem, anxiety, and depression, and are more likely to live in negative home situations characterized by domestic violence and low social support from marital partners. Each of these factors can influence a mother's capacity to parent her children, and combined create a toxic brew for them in the home. The same can be said for addicted fathers caring for children.

The quality of the serve and return relationship diminishes when parents are under stress. Further, addictions and the stressors that accompany them greatly reduce the chances of a nurturing relationship fostered by healthy serve and return. Generally, children who find emotional nurturance in their relationships with their mothers show more positive outcomes and even appeared to compensate for home troubles (like alcoholism and other addictions) by high achievement in school.[108]

Alcoholism appears to affect parents' relationships with teenagers in much the same way depression does (see chapter 4). A recent study compared co-operative and problem-solving abilities among families from three groups: fathers suffering from depression, fathers suffering from alcoholism, and fathers who were non-distressed (that is, exhibiting no symptoms of depression or addiction). Non-distressed families performed best, but the alcoholic- and depressed-father families were the same in how congenial and capable they were of solving the problem under discussion.[109]

In another study of teenagers, the negative effect of parental alcoholism in either parent was reduced when the teen reported a positive serve and return relationship (see chapter 2) with one of their parents — more secure attachment and better communication helped overcome some of the negative effects on the teen's self-esteem. Similar effects pertain to children of illicit drug-abusing parents. While teenagers of substance-abusing parents are at risk of substance abuse themselves, this happens most often when the teenager has a history of being neglected by his or her parents.[110]

Researchers have speculated that the kind of attachment adults had with their parents, of whom at least one was a substance abuser, can explain the difficulty that married couples raised by addicts have. Taken together, these findings suggest that promoting a secure attachment, characterized by healthy serve and return relationships, may be one way to overcome the effects of addiction on children.

SCORES ON THE ALCOHOL AND DRUG USE SURVEY

Low Risk (Score: 0)

Congratulations! Neither alcohol nor drug abuse appear to be a problem for you.

John finishes the questionnaire, scoring zero. He double-checks his answers, probing each response to make sure he isn't kidding himself. He heaves a sigh of relief. The ache in his skull recedes. Next time, he'll keep it to one or two drinks, even if it means ducking out on his staff during their after-work outings. *Some things are more important,* he says to himself, as images of Sandy and Bo flash in his mind.

Moderate Risk (Score: 1–4)

If you scored between 1 and 4 on the questionnaire, your behaviour has raised some red flags. There is a good chance that your drinking or drug use has had some impact on your relationships and parenting.

Health officials advise that women should consume no more than ten drinks a week and two drinks a day, and men should consume no more than fifteen drinks a week and three drinks a day. If you exceed this limit or feel otherwise concerned about your drinking/drug use, I recommend you reach out to an alcohol and/or addiction counsellor to explore ways to reduce your risk. There are usually confidential supports available through the workplace, or your family doctor or nurse practitioner can recommend a resource for you. You can also find resources in your community by searching online using terms such as *Alcoholics Anonymous* or *drug abuse* and the name of your town/city/region. Books are also available on how to give up alcohol, such as *Alcohol: How to Give It Up and Be Glad You Did* by Philip Tate.

John scores 3 on the test — most of the questions whizzed by easily, but numbers 3 through 5 nailed him.

There was no doubt that his drinking bothered Sandy, and Bo was getting old enough to catch wind of it, too. Quitting after two drinks was a challenge, one he lost more often than he won. And he felt guilty most mornings when he'd over-indulged the night before.

"Enough is enough," he mumbles, queuing up his employee portal from work. He looks up the confidential number for counselling and sets up an appointment for that evening.

High Risk (Score: 5 or More)

If you scored 5 or more, you need to get help immediately. Your drinking and/or drug abuse not only puts you at high risk for a number of serious diseases, including cancer and heart disease,[111,112] but also likely affects your relationships with co-workers, friends, and family. Unfortunately, a score in this range suggests a near certain probability of impeding your serve and return relationships with your children, putting them at risk for a host of long-term ailments. It is imperative that you seek help as soon as possible.

Counselling is a helpful tool in addressing addiction. Talk to your family doctor or nurse practitioner to find out about the counselling options available in your community. You may want to speak to a counsellor who is accessed privately (for example, through a local privately funded clinic that is either recommended to you or discovered by yourself); via your employer (through an employee assistance program, if you have one); or via publically funded services and physician referrals (available in most Western nations, except the U.S.). Often these programs are publicly funded and can be accessed for little or no charge. For instance, Ontario Addiction Treatment Centres operate in over fifty cities across the province and offer methadone treatments, addiction counselling, and HIV care through the province's public health insurance program.

If you also received a high score in the questionnaire assessing trauma (chapter 1), I recommend you find a counsellor who specializes in people who have experienced early adversity, as your addiction may stem from negative experiences in childhood. In this case, *trauma-informed care* or *trauma-informed therapy* may be the search terms you need to use if you are seeking resources online. As suggested above, under Moderate Risk, Alcoholics Anonymous or its equivalent (available for most forms of drug addiction) can provide a safe and supportive environment for overcoming your addiction. Many programs are run in cities and smaller communities throughout the world.

Once you have reached out for help with your addiction, consider again how your addiction is affecting your children and your relationship with them. I recommend you reach out to a counsellor who can assist you in repairing and enriching the quality of your serve and return relationships with your children. You will be giving your children the gift of resiliency. I urge you to review chapter 2 for details.

You should also work toward any needed reparations in your relationship with your marital partner, if you have one. A healthy marital relationship can also contribute to the resiliency of you, your partner, and your children. See chapter 8 for details.

John sighs. The screen beams the questionnaire results up at him. He scored a 7. It was at once the biggest shock of his life and the most obvious possible outcome. Had he really needed a questionnaire to tell him he had a problem? Yet somehow he had. It had always been too easy to explain his behaviour with a mixture of self-deprecation and pride. He'd been a big drinker since college, when he could drink more than men twice his size and still make it to class at eight the next morning. In a way he felt like the same punk kid, but he was approaching middle age now, and while his capacity might not have changed, his ability to bounce back the next morning certainly had.

The divorce should have woken him up. It was his drinking that killed his marriage, after all. He'd as good as shoved a bottle down its throat and drowned it with liquor. Yet it was always so easy to blame Stacey. *She's uptight. She's too clingy. She's always cutting me down in front of my mom and dad and brother.* That the "cutting down" was mostly pleas for them to help her curb his drinking seemed easy to ignore in the moment, less so now.

But if anything could get through to him, it was his children. Sandy's disgust and Bo's hurt had come together like oil and flame, igniting a beacon that cut through the fog and straight to the heart of him. He might be high-functioning enough to do his job well — he still prided himself on that, however perversely — but to parent well, he needed to be dry.

John checked his calendar and saw a check-up scheduled with his family doctor next month. He called the office and asked to have it bumped up to next week. He'd lay the whole thing bare and see what the doctor had to say. There had to be something out there to help him.

Chapter 6

Abuse and Violence

Let's raise children who won't have to
recover from their childhoods.

— Pam Leo

Asha steps through the sliding glass doors and into
the emergency room. The lobby attacks her senses
with its brightness, awash in white tile and polished
chrome. She blinks at the brightness, then her nostrils
are invaded by clouds of antiseptic draped ineffectually
over old blood and bile and fear.

Her breath catches as if all the air was suddenly
removed from the emergency room. She's unsure if
it's from her confusing tangle of feelings — pain, anxiety, fear, and hope — or if her ribs are broken along
with the purpling bruises on her neck and left shoulder.

With her next breath, more pain lashes her, and Asha lurches forward into the emergency room, painfully jostling her thirteen-year-old son, Ari.

His right arm in her unbreakable maternal grip, Ari protests mildly, his face marred by misery and his voice barely a whisper. "Hey, Ma, ow! Slow down."

As Asha pauses to regain her balance, Ari tightens his grip on his left arm, holding it protectively against his body. *He's big for his age, but still a child*, thinks Asha sadly. For all his effort, it is apparent that he is unable to contain the pain emanating from his injured shoulder.

A small pang of guilt drops into her belly at the thought she might've caused her son a bit more pain, however inadvertently. But it's quickly washed away by her worry and sense of urgency. *My baby is hurt!* she telegraphs mentally to the emergency room staff as she takes a number and the two of them wait their turn to be seen.

The ER isn't busy, thankfully, and soon a nurse calls their number. Asha insists they be seen together, as she doesn't want him to leave her side. They shuffle to an examination room, where another nurse recites a litany of questions. Another nurse appears with something for their pain. After that, a pair of aids lead Ari away for his x-ray, and while Asha waits for her turn, the nurse sits down across from her and flips open a clipboard. She tells Asha that at this hospital, it is standard procedure to screen everyone who comes in with a physical injury for signs of domestic abuse.

THE DOMESTIC ABUSE SURVEY

The following questions are routinely asked of adults to assess abuse and violence in the family. Take the survey now and then see the end of the chapter for your results and recommended resources.

Domestic Abuse Risk Survey

1. Are you currently in an abusive marital or intimate relationship (includes physical, sexual, and emotional abuse)?

Yes _____ No _____

2. With your child(ren), do you or another caregiver regularly engage in physical punishment, ignore them or their needs, or say things that hurt their feelings, because they deserve it?

Yes _____ No _____

Score of 0: read *low risk*
Score of 1–2: read *high risk*

WHAT DO WE MEAN BY ABUSE?

According to the Centers for Disease Control and Prevention, child abuse is defined as "any act of commission or omission by a parent or other caregiver that results in harm, potential for harm, or threat of harm to a child." This includes physical, sexual, and psychological forms of abuse. The same criteria apply for domestic violence between former or current partners. Neglect is considered a form of abuse and treated with equal seriousness.

HOW COMMON IS ABUSE?

In chapter 1, we covered the ACE study. In addition to revealing illuminating correlations between the presence of ACEs and adverse outcomes, the study's findings also provided an insightful look at the prevalence of child abuse and neglect as well as violence between parents over time. Over seventeen thousand adults (nearly eight thousand men and over nine thousand women) participated in the 2008 study, of whom a surprising number recounted histories of various forms of abuse:

- thirteen percent of women and eight percent of men recalled emotional abuse
- twenty-seven percent of women and thirty percent of men recalled physical abuse
- twenty-five percent of women and sixteen percent of men recalled sexual abuse
- seventeen percent of women and twelve percent of men recalled emotional neglect
- nine percent of women and eleven percent of men recalled physical neglect
- fourteen percent of women and twelve percent of men recalled violence against their mother

The average age of these participants was fifty-seven years; seventy-five percent were Caucasian, seventy-five percent had attended college, and all participants had jobs and good health care, placing the cohort in a lower than average risk group for experiencing violence. This suggests that the prevalence of abuse and inter-partner violence is, if anything, more severe than reported. International data reflect these findings. The WHO reports that rates of severe child physical punishment, such as hitting the child with an object, range from four percent (Chile and the U.S.) to thirty-six percent (India), while rates of moderate physical punishment such as spanking range from forty-seven percent (U.S.) to seventy-five percent (Philippines).

With respect to abuse in marital or intimate partner relationships, in 2013 the WHO reported on a variety of families from low-, middle-, and high-income countries in Africa, North and South America, the Middle East, Europe, South-East Asia, and the Western Pacific. They found that thirty percent of all women experienced physical and/or sexual abuse by their partner. Alarmingly, this number was not significantly lower in high-income countries, with twenty-three percent of women in Australia, Canada, Denmark, the United Kingdom, Japan, and New Zealand reporting abuse at the hands of their partners.

Abuse of male partners in intimate relationships is also a problem; however, rates of such abuse are difficult to estimate as men are far less likely to report it. Studies conducted between 2000 and 2010 from England, Wales, Ireland, the United States, and Canada suggest rates of violence against men at the hands of their female partners ranged between three percent and seven percent.[113–16]

Perhaps most troubling is that most women who report abuse by their partner are of child-bearing age. In Canada, for example, fifty-six percent of abused women are between the ages of eighteen and thirty-four, and the WHO showed that rates of abuse range from thirty-one percent to thirty-eight percent for women aged twenty to forty-four years. As well, preschool children under five years of age are disproportionately overrepresented in households where women experience abuse.[117] Moreover, women exposed to this abuse are sixteen percent more likely to have babies with low birth weights (linked to a host of health problems and lifelong challenges) and twice as likely to experience depression.

CHILD ABUSE AND NEGLECT

Given the psychological, cognitive, and physical health effects of abuse, the Harvard Center on the Developing child has described exposure to abuse, inflicted directly to the child or witnessed by them, as a "toxic stressor" to children's development. The risks of abuse are not simply for injury during or in the immediate aftermath of an attack, but continue years after the imminent threat may have vanished.

I discussed briefly the Romanian orphans in chapter 2. Their tragic experiences describe one of the most profound cases of neglect in modern times. The after-effects of their mistreatment pervaded every domain of development, including social, emotional, mental, cognitive, and physical, with many affected children diagnosed as "failure to thrive" (that is, failing to gain weight or achieve developmental milestones like rolling, sitting up unsupported, or talking as expected). Children from the Romanian orphan cohort were frequently shorter than their peers, while their brains were both smaller in volume and had reduced connectivity, meaning the network of synapses that allow the brain to function was thinner and less robust. While outcomes this extreme are thankfully uncommon, similar effects on a smaller scale have been found among children who have been subjected to less profound forms of abuse and neglect.[118]

More commonplace examples in the Western world involve corporal punishment, such as spanking. An immense body of research has examined the impact of corporal punishment on child development. While corporal punishment produces immediate compliance in children, it also raises their levels of aggression, resulting in greater likelihood of aggressive or violent behaviour. Corporal punishment also has long-term effects on mental health, increasing the child's likelihood of experiencing depression in adolescence,[119] and leads to delinquent, criminal, and antisocial behaviour.

Essentially, corporal punishment erodes the quality of parent–child relationships, negating opportunities for the serve and return interactions so essential to child development. Corporal punishment teaches children that parents are sources of pain rather than knowledge and reduces their desire to go to their parents for support, guidance, or answers to their questions about the world.[120] In perhaps the most comprehensive and up-to-date review published,[121] findings from 162 studies including 160,927 children revealed that spanking did not differ from physical abuse in its effects on detrimental outcomes, including

- low moral internalization
- child aggression
- chid antisocial behaviour
- child externalizing behavioural problems (aggression, hyperactivity)
- child internalizing behavioural problems (depression, anxiety, shyness)
- child mental health problems
- negative parent–child relationships
- impaired cognitive ability
- low self-esteem
- adult antisocial behaviour
- adult mental health problems
- adult support for physical punishment.

While controversial, another less comprehensive review conducted in 2013 suggests that the effects of corporal punishment may be more trivial than thought, with rather small effects on aggression, hyperactivity, depression, social withdrawal and cognitive performance. The more negative effects of corporal punishment were attributed to various other factors, including

- harsh delivery, such as punching or kicking or using a weapon, resulting in bruising or injury;
- lack of parental communication about reasons for the punishment;
- an absence of healthy serve and return relationships to temper the physical discipline,[122] especially from mothers; and
- both mothers and fathers delivering corporal punishment.[123]

Nonetheless, researchers continue to advise parents against using corporal punishment.[124] I agree with this assessment. As a parent myself, I would much rather preserve the quality of my relationship with my child, so that I can continue to rely on this trusted serve and return relationship into the future, than try to force my child's compliance today.

EXPOSURE OF CHILDREN TO INTER-PARENTAL ABUSE

With respect to exposure to inter-parental violence, over thirty years of research has shown that exposure to violence between parents predicts children's maladjustment and poor psychosocial outcomes.[125–33] It impacts children's likelihood of developing

- insecure attachment (see Chapter 3: Serve and Return Parenting) in infants and preschoolers;

- depression, anxiety, and angry outbursts, worsening over time as children grow older;
- aggressive behaviour directed towards peers, parents, and siblings;
- atypical or maladaptive behaviours in young children (such as making odd sounds or repetitive movements);
- difficulty in establishing and maintaining interpersonal relationships;
- reduced self-esteem in school-age children and into adulthood;
- emotion regulation and executive functioning problems, which include reduced abilities in planning, organization, and task completion;
- cognitive problems, such as reduced IQ, academic and learning problems, poorer memory function, and verbal problems;
- physical health problems, such as eating, sleeping, pain problems, asthma, and allergies;
- trauma and post-traumatic stress disorder (PTSD) symptoms such as dissociation, which includes selective memory loss, self-detachment, and distorted perception of reality;
- digestive problems and headaches;
- bedwetting, weight problems, and obesity;
- self-harm and talk about suicide, as well as suicide ideation, and suicidal behaviour;
- accelerated telomere (that is, the caps at the end of each strand of DNA that protect our

chromosomes from deterioration) length decline, which is linked to cardiovascular disease, obesity, and diabetes in later life; and

- glucocorticoid receptor changes, operating in the hypothalamic-pituitary-adrenal axis or the stress response system to alter the levels of the stress-hormone cortisol (at high levels cortisol is neurotoxic and damaging to the brain and body organs).

Children exposed to inter-parental abuse, usually against their mothers, face as great a risk for adverse outcomes as children who were abused themselves,[134] while both witnessing *and* experiencing abuse compounds its effects, especially when mothers are the abusers.[135] Length of exposure to abuse is closely tied to the severity of its impact,[136,137] but the timing also plays an important role. Children exposed to abuse during the preschool years are most at risk, and the effects are more damaging in the short and long term. These children demonstrate more emotional and internalizing behavioural problems,[138,139] social problems (for example, social inhibition, antisocial behaviour), developmental delays,[140,141] aggression, and less verbal and cognitive abilities by standardized norms than children who are exposed to abuse at a younger (during infancy) or older age (in elementary or high school).

To put these many findings in perspective, one classic study of preschoolers raised in families in which their father abused their mother showed that compared to children in non-abusive families, these children demonstrated more behavioural problems including aggression and violence with peers, difficult temperaments, and less ability to appropriately respond to everyday situations with their playgroup peers or caregivers. They also had more challenging relationships with their caregivers in the playgroup, including fighting with or avoiding their caregivers.[142] Children who witnessed the violence against their mother were the worst off. Mothers who were emotionally abused (compared to physically abused) and who suffered from low self-esteem had children who demonstrated the most behavioural problems.

PROTECTION FROM THE STORM

Fortunately, even in the most severe cases of abuse, there is reason for hope. Some children from abusive families develop well or are "resilient" in spite of this risk. Many children escape from abusive environments and go on to lead happy, fulfilling lives. This variability is thought to relate to parents' ability to establish emotionally safe and secure environments for children to grow and develop optimally.[143] Two rival theories[144] help explain how exposure to inter-parental abuse can affect some children but spare others and offer ideas for ways to promote resilience.

First, the spillover theory suggests that the stress a parent (usually mother) experiences due to abuse will negatively impact her parenting behaviour. Second, the compensatory theory suggests that parents may invest more in a relationship with their child to make up for exposure to domestic abuse. There is support for both theories: When parents (especially mothers) engaged in harsh discipline, the spillover theory is supported, and children are likely to fare poorly. For example, children exposed to both abuse between their parents and parent–child aggression, especially mother–child aggression, demonstrate more serious adjustment difficulties.

However, when mothers are warm and nurturing in interactions with their children, in spite of the abuse exposure, their children do better. My own research supports this observation. In a study of mothers who had left their abusive partner, fellow researchers and I asked the participants questions about how they coped with the abuse. We also measured the quality of their serve and return relationship as well as their children's development. Mothers whose children fared best reported that they compensated for their children's exposure to abuse by being extremely sensitive and responsive to them. For example, one mother said, "I tried to cuddle her more and stuff like that because of everything she had to see." Another mother said, "I would try and teach her things and read her books and sing to her and spend a lot of time with her." So, in general, healthy serve and return relationships with mothers have been found to contribute to this resiliency, buffering the influence of exposure to domestic abuse.

Mothers need to be mentally well to contribute to healthy serve and return relationships. Mental wellness acts as a protective factor that predicts better emotion regulation and social-emotional behaviour in children, in spite of exposure to inter-parental abuse.[145] In contrast, mothers in abusive relationships who suffered from depression or other mental health issues are less able to insulate their children from the effects of their environment.[146]

More involvement from mothers, a key characteristic of healthy serve and return relationships, even reduces the risk for asthma in children exposed to abuse.[147] This connection may seem less intuitive than most, but researchers have pinpointed a possible mechanism that could drive this change. When forced to adapt to high stress environments, many children exist in a constant state of heightened physiological arousal, which can play havoc with their immune responses and hence increase the risk for asthma. An involved mother or other parental figure can offer a soothing counterweight, lowering how stressful the environment is overall and, in turn, facilitating more measured immune responses in the child.[148,149]

In addition to parents, other close relationships, including friends, family, and professionals, can provide a similar protective influence (see chapter 8). These individuals can provide emotional support, education, and financial resources, which can lower symptoms of depression in women who experience abuse from partners (see chapter 3), thereby buffering the impact of abuse on depression (see chapter 4). This in turn allows mothers to engage in healthier serve and return interactions with their children, which can promote resilience.

Children can also establish serve and return relationships with individuals outside of their parents. Serve and return behaviours practised among siblings[150-51] or extended family members[152] may also significantly decrease the risk for maladjustment. Supportive peer relationships may also play a role.[153]

Higher self-esteem in children exposed to abuse between their parents is also associated with greater resilience or fewer adjustment problems.[154-55] Child temperament,[156] or how easy-going the child is, can also predict better developmental outcomes. The child's attribution of self-blame and guilt concerning the violence,[157] spirituality and emotional intelligence,[158] empathy, self-regulation, and self-esteem,[159] as well as involvement in after-school activities[160] have all been shown to make a difference. Socio-economic advantage, including family and neighbourhood characteristics can also promote resiliency. Exposure to abuse thus has significant impacts throughout childhood and into adult life; however, some children persist in doing well despite their challenging circumstances.

SCORES ON THE DOMESTIC ABUSE SURVEY

Low Risk (Score: 0)

While the other sections in this book employ three levels of risk — low, moderate, and high — research on violence and abuse suggests the absence of a grey area. Even a small exposure can potentially have a severe effect, and as such I have included only two categories: low risk (that is, no exposure to violence or abuse) and high risk (any exposure to violence or abuse).

If you scored 0, that is terrific! This is not a risk factor for you, your parenting, or your child(ren)'s development.

Asha listens to the questions with surprise. Raising an eyebrow, she says, "My husband has never raised a hand to me in twenty years of marriage. And we discipline our children sternly, but without violence. Just as I told you, our car slipped on the ice and we hit a tree on the way to school this morning. That is the truth. My husband will be here soon and you can ask him, too, if you want."

"That's all we wanted to hear," the nurse says, tucking the form away with a reassuring smile. "Thanks so much for your honesty. Sometimes people just need to be asked and we want to be sure that everyone has the chance to get the help they need."

"Of course," Asha says, softening. The questions had caught her off guard, but she supposes it was better for them to be asked. *If it helps one woman leave a violent situation,* she thinks, *then it's worth the discomfort for the rest of us.*

Ari returns, his arm in a sling. He gives his mother a sheepish smile. She kisses his cheek as she puts a sheltering arm around him, knowing that this experience is literally just a bump in the road.

High Risk (Score: 1 or 2)

If you scored 1 or 2, help is needed. If you are in immediate danger, contact your local women's emergency shelter or crisis intervention services to get help from trained family violence service providers, who can get you to a safe and secure location. While less widely available, similar resources are available to men. Search for these resources online, using the search terms *women's emergency shelter* or *women's crisis intervention* (or the same terms without *women's*, if you are a man) and the name of your town/city/region to find twenty-four hour helplines with access to counselling and resources. Typically, hospital emergency rooms can also connect you with a social worker with expertise in family violence, who can help you plan for your safety. Most communities have such emergency housing or access to emergency housing in nearby communities. If you do not have such access to any of these resources, you should contact your local police and find a safe, secure location. It may be a hotel, or a friend or family member's home. Regardless, you need to connect to family violence service providers through some means. Police services frequently have their own victim services workers who are often social workers with expertise in family violence.

Typical family violence service providers are specially trained and experienced in working with victims of family violence. They understand, for example, about how the cycle of violence works to keep abused mothers in the couple relationship. While in the cycle, after the abuse episode, the abuser is typically very contrite, says they will change their behaviour, and seeks forgiveness. The mother then forgives her partner and the cycle starts over again, ultimately culminating in another abusive episode. This pattern lulls women into having false hope and effectively keeps them in the abusive environment. Knowing this pattern ensures that service providers are non-judgemental and empathetic, as they understand this and other dynamics that underpin the victim's reasons for staying. These service providers will support you by understanding your situation and can keep you and your children safe because they have the knowledge to enact many safeguards, such as keeping your contact with them confidential and private. Further, once you are in the system and out of danger, these service providers can connect you to the other supports you need, such as longer-term housing subsidies, counselling and therapy for your children, and job training.

If you are not in immediate danger, you need to reach out to your family physician, nurse practitioner, public health nurse, or a counsellor for advice. Contacting your employee assistance program, if available, may also be advisable. Any of these contacts should be able to connect you with the appropriate resources in your community.

Ideally, your partner will voluntarily undergo counselling or family therapy. If not, discussing your options with local abuse experts is the best course of action. If the abuse is in the past but you are concerned about your child, counselling is essential to help mitigate any self-blame the child may feel, to build self-esteem, and to deal directly with the potential negative outcomes of the exposure (for example, aggressive tendencies). While child and family counselling services are available in most communities, services may also be available for your child through his or her school. I urge you to reach out to your child's teacher who can potentially refer you to additional school-based resources and work with you to support your child's resilience.

Try searching online for local resources by using the terms *victims services* or *family violence shelters* and the name of your town/city/region. To ensure that women and children in shelters are kept safe from their assailants, the addresses of the shelters are not published. However, they typically can be contacted by phone on family violence helplines, twenty-four hours a day. Many programs and shelters offer extensive resources including services for children and youth, information about how to navigate the court system, family and men's counselling, information on healthy relationships, and access to emergency shelter and longer-term housing support. Some examples include the following:

- Public Health Agency of Canada: www.canada. ca/en/public-health/services/health-promotion/ stop-family-violence.html
- Women's Aid (U.K.): www.nationaldomesticviolencehelpline.org.uk
- National Coalition Against Domestic Violence (NCADV) (U.S.): www.ncadv.org
- Australian Domestic and Family Violence Clearinghouse : www.snaicc.org.au/australian-domestic-family-violence-clearinghouse-website

If you are concerned about preventing parental violence and abuse against your children, specific parenting programs are available to help. Triple P (Positive Parenting Program) offers insight on positive discipline strategies to help parents avoid spanking, the Nurturing Parenting Program, a series of courses designed by a leading expert in child abuse and neglect, builds nurturing parenting skills in order to break the cycle of violence that spans across generations. Courses taught one on one or in small groups are available in cities across North America, and online courses allow access worldwide.

Many parenting books cover positive discipline as an alternative to physical means of discipline. You can find any number of books on positive discipline. Jane Nelson has written numerous titles, any of which I would recommend. Using this search term online, you can also find great web resources, such as the Positive Discipline Association: Developing Respectful Relationships website (https://positivediscipline.org).

Use all the resources at your disposal to address the abuse you are experiencing or to help you parent more effectively using positive discipline practices. In fact, some suggest that availability and accessibility of social support resources in your community have the greatest impact on promoting resilience.

Asha feels her face go pale. Her breath catches again, perhaps on a broken rib, perhaps on fear. The fear is an ugly, cold sensation, as if she were bleeding slowly from a deep, unbearable wound. The nurse flips through her chart, tactfully allowing Asha as much time as she needs to respond to the questions.

As her breath returns, the word *no* rises instinctively to Asha's lips. It poises on the tip of her tongue, a high diver ready for another clean, deceitful leap. At the last second, the truth belly flops out instead. "Yes," she says, her voice flat. "He has hurt me for years, but never the children. Not until today. The children didn't know. He only lashed out when they were asleep or at school. Mostly he does it when we argue. Today, Raj thought Ari had already left for school. He overhead us arguing and he stepped in…." Asha breaks off and covers her face, now in tears.

The nurse takes Asha's hand and asks more questions. "When was the last time he struck you?"

"Last month," she says sadly, remembering.

"Have you been hurt badly enough before to require medical treatment?"

"Yes, but I said I slipped on the stairs. No one knew the truth," Asha answers honestly for the first time. After that first lurching syllable with which she acknowledged her pain, the words begin flowing effortlessly. She finds it a relief to discuss it with somebody, anybody.

"We need to connect you to the hospital social worker. Is that okay with you? She is experienced in this kind of situation and will connect you with the community resources you need to keep you and your children safe," the nurse says matter-of-factly.

"I … I don't know. Will the social worker call the police? I don't want to get my husband in trouble. He just needs help."

"No," the nurse responds. "We won't call the police unless you want us to. We just want you and your kids to be safe."

Asha agrees to wait for the social worker to see her. Meanwhile the nurse provides Asha with the names of some resources for women and children affected by violence. They are listed on a sticky note-sized paper that she re-rolls and slides into a hollow lipstick container, designed to conceal help of this kind for women like her. Fighting back more tears, Asha takes it with a nod of thanks.

"I'm not sure I'm ready to leave my husband," Asha says, recovering from the shock of what she had finally revealed. The nurse nods understandingly. She hands Asha a box of tissues. They wait together in silence.

"Do you think your husband would go to counselling?" the nurse asks.

Here Asha once again hesitates. Raj in counselling? He's such a private person, she has a hard time picturing it. But when they had married fourteen years ago, she didn't think he was the type to descend to violence, either. "I … I'm not sure," she says.

Noticing her hesitation, the nurse says again reassuringly, "When the social worker arrives, she will help you figure out your options. Okay?"

"Okay," says Asha, just as Ari swings open the door.

Chapter 7

Reflective Function

We began to think that changes in a relationship are often the result of changes in a parent's capacity to make sense of her child as a separate, differentiated person with thoughts, feelings, and a mind of his own — to think more reflectively about that child.

— Arietta Slade

"Thank you so much. Goodbye," says Michelle. Her shoulders slumped, she looks down as she fumbles with shaking fingers to press "end call" on her cellphone. As she lifts her head, she says flatly, "They found Bryden."

Jim grabs her by the shoulders. It's a comforting gesture but also a steadying one. "Where?"

"At the bus station."

Jim sighs with relief. "Thank God he didn't make it far."

"No," she says, holding back a sob. "The bus station in Montreal."

"Montreal? How'd he make it all the way to Montreal? What bus driver would let a fourteen-year-old board the bus alone like that? Where'd he even get the money?"

Michelle shakes her head. "I don't know." She thinks of the conspicuous gap on her nightstand this morning, the spot where she keeps a collection of coins and small bills. Stealing! She brushes the thought aside, not quite ready to voice it to Jim. "At least he's safe. They're taking him to Marc's house. Apparently Marc's mom thought we'd okayed the visit. And Jim, he says he's not coming home!"

She can hold back her tears no longer. Sobbing, she clutches Jim, who rubs her back and murmurs reassuring words in her ear. Michelle appreciates his support, but can process none of what he says. Her mind turns as ever to Bryden and this awful metamorphosis that has so suddenly overtaken him.

She knows the divorce was tough on him, but that had all happened years ago, and he seemed to have handled it with the quiet maturity she knew and loved in him. He and Jim had always gotten on well together, and while the move to Toronto brought a lot of major life changes with it, it's not as if they'd gone to live in a foreign country. Bryden has cousins in Toronto that he'd practically grown up with, and Michelle had always been more than willing to coordinate visits from his Montreal friends.

Yet somehow, without her knowing, it had all gone wrong. Something in Bryden had changed. Stealing, lying, and now this sudden burst of defiance. She can't reconcile this behaviour with the sweet boy she knows, the angel who never has a mean word for anyone, whose worst infraction before today was collecting a wounded baby squirrel and nursing it in their garage without telling her.

* * *

The psychologist's office is warm and homey, its clinical function tempered with potted plants and beige carpeting. A pair of floor lamps provide gentle illumination without the harsh buzz of fluorescent lights. The room feels more like part of someone's home than a doctor's office, which Michelle supposes is the point. But the warmest décor in the world cannot alleviate the chill radiating towards her from her son, who sits on the couch beside her, arms crossed over his narrow chest.

"So, Bryden," says Dr. Saunders. "How are you doing this morning?"

"Fine," says Bryden, his tone suggesting he is anything but. It is the first word Michelle has heard him speak since he returned home a week before, his voice sounding almost foreign to her ears.

Dr. Saunders works Bryden for a few more minutes, extracting a few terse sentences that are, for all their brevity, minor miracles in Michelle's eyes. After that she turns to Michelle and begins asking some questions.

THE REFLECTIVE FUNCTION SURVEY

The following questions were devised by me to assess reflective function, based on my expert understanding of the key concepts and how they affect relationships with children. Take the survey now and then see the end of the chapter for your results and recommended resources.

Reflective Function Survey

1. Can you accurately name your feelings as you are experiencing them?

Yes _____ No _____

2. Are you able to see how your thoughts and feelings affect your actions?

Yes _____ No _____

3. Can you accurately imagine others' thoughts and feelings and see how they affect their actions?

Yes _____ No _____

4. Can you accurately imagine your child's thoughts and feelings and see how they affect their actions?

Yes _____ No _____

Tally total number of "yes" answers:

Score 4: read *low risk*

Score 1–3: read *moderate risk*

Score 0: read *high risk*

WHAT IS REFLECTIVE FUNCTION?

We learned earlier that exposure to parental violence, depression, and addictions have a toxic effect on children's development by reducing parents' sensitivity and responsiveness to their children. This impedes their ability to form effective serve and return relationships, which are essential to building the secure parent–child attachments necessary for healthy child development.

Serve and return relationships are also influenced by parents' reflective function (RF), which is the uniquely human capacity to understand and make sense of one's own and others' behaviours by considering underlying mental states — specifically emotions, feelings, thoughts, intentions, desires, or wishes.[161] Emotions and feelings can include anger, sadness, happiness, guilt, agitation, and frustration. RF involves noticing and attending to mental states in yourself and others and interpreting another person's behaviour through your understanding of their mental states.[162] With respect to parents, those with high RF have the ability to see their child as an independent person with a mind of their own, complete with emotions, feelings, thoughts, and intentions.

More generally, parental RF demonstrates parents' capacity to understand their children. Parental RF is thus defined as the parent's ability to envision the child's mental states and to conceive of the child as a psychological agent whose behaviour and actions are motivated by these mental states. While RF enables the adult to regulate his or her feelings, thoughts, and behaviour in general, parental RF enables the parent to regulate his or her feelings, thoughts, and behaviour in relation to the child.[163]

Consider, for example, a crying preschooler: A highly reflective parent would be able to recognize and address the source of the child's distress by considering what may be in the child's mind, while a poorly reflective parent would possibly ignore or misinterpret the source of the child's distress.

RF is similar to, but not the same as, a lot of related ideas captured in terms such as *mindfulness, empathy, insightfulness, theory of mind,* and *emotional intelligence.* Experts even say that many of these related ideas may tap into the same underlying neurobiological socio-cognitive system as RF.[164] The concept that may be most familiar is emotional intelligence, which refers to a person's ability to perceive, control, and evaluate emotions. Parental RF includes this capacity, alongside the ability to understand others' and your own thoughts, and to recognize that others (especially children) have minds of their own, with their own unique mental states (that is, feelings, thoughts, and intentions).

HOW DOES REFLECTIVE FUNCTION RELATE TO CHILDREN'S DEVELOPMENT?

We learned earlier that healthy serve and return relationships are related to healthy child development outcomes and can even overcome the stressors in the environment that can undermine children's healthy development. We will now look at how RF contributes to healthy child development, both directly and indirectly through serve and return relationships. To clarify, while RF is an internal ability, healthy serve and return relationships are noticeable by behavioural responses of parents to their child's cues. In this way, healthy serve and return relationships are underpinned by RF.

Parents begin demonstrating RF almost immediately after their children are born, as it influences how they react to their infant's cues. For example:

- After noticing his baby's interest in curling her small hand around his finger, the father repositions his newborn daughter so that she does not have to reach for dad's finger to hold it.
- After noticing the buckles on her six-month-old daughter's overalls are irritating her, the mom changes her daughter into another outfit, offering sympathetic vocalizations to show she understands.
- A father notices his hungry one-year-old son is too overwhelmed by the noise of a family gathering to eat, so he takes the baby to a quieter spot, showing in word, tone, and action that he understands his son's emotions, even if he himself is not experiencing the feeling of being overwhelmed and hungry.

These scenarios demonstrate the theory behind how RF is believed to influence child development, beginning from the earliest interactions with young babies. It involves concepts called "marking" and "affect mirroring."[165]

When responding to the baby's cues (that is, when they return the serve), mothers and fathers intuitively mark their response to show the baby that they are noticing and listening. Further, when marking, parents use affect mirroring to show the baby that they understand their baby's underlying mental state, thought, or intention. For example, when babies cry and parents sympathize by saying, for example, "Ooh, there now," they mark their response, and should do so by adopting vocal and facial expressions that reflect but do not exactly mimic the baby's crying. Through this behaviour, parents mark that they recognize and sympathize with the baby's emotion, but in a way that the baby knows the parent is not truly experiencing the emotion him- or herself. In other words, parents mark that they notice the baby's serve and mirror the baby's emotion (affect) but not exactly, showing that they recognize the emotion but that they are not actually experiencing it themselves.

Marking and affect mirroring tell the child (unconsciously, of course) that the parent is not feeling the baby's feeling, *but understands it*. The extension of this idea is that the baby learns (again, unconsciously) that he can affect his environment but is separate from others in it. The baby perceives that her mind can be understood, but that others have different minds and emotional states from her and are separate individuals from her. This experience is thought to help the child learn to differentiate themselves from others.

In contrast, parents who exactly mirror the child's emotion — for instance, by bursting into tears when their child is crying — prevent the child from learning that they have a mind of their own. This can happen when parents are overwhelmed by stress and are not coping well with parenting. For example, a frustrated, fatigued, or depressed parent may indeed cry in response to their child crying. The parent's frustration and fatigue with managing their child can create responses that are not affect mirroring, but rather perceived as scary or confusing to the child. Babies will learn that if they feel sad, scared, or tired, others will feel exactly as they do.

Attending this idea is the child's (unconscious) realization that seeking out comfort and soothing will not likely be effective or calming. Rather, the child will be confused by his or her apparent ability to create/cause the same emotion in other people. So, rather than being a safe haven from stress, parents become an echo chamber, bouncing back the child's emotions, thoughts, and intentions. As Peter Fonagy and his fellow experts in RF said best:

> A display that is congruent with the baby's state, but lacks markedness may overwhelm the infant. It is felt to be the parent's own real emotion, making the infant's experience seem contagious, or universal ... the infant's perception of a corresponding but realistic negative emotion is likely to escalate rather than regulate the infant's state, leading to traumatization.

The inability to differentiate one's own emotions and thoughts from those of others is linked to a host of mental health problems, especially personality disorders.[166]

PARENTAL REFLECTIVE FUNCTION AND CHILDREN'S DEVELOPMENT

Higher RF-related abilities of mothers and fathers have been linked to children's

- ability to imagine what another person thinks or believes[167]
- recognition that other people have perspectives that are different from their own[168–71]
- social-emotional adjustment
- attachment security to their mothers as babies.[172]

Lower RF-related abilities in mothers and fathers have been linked to children's

- internalizing behaviours such as mood and anxiety problems
- externalizing behaviours such as aggression and conduct problems.

CAN PARENTS LEARN REFLECTIVE FUNCTION?

Fortunately, research shows that RF can be learned. Typically, intervention programs have involved help by a psychologist, psychiatrist, or trained mental health professional. But group parenting programs such as Circle of Security and Watch, Wait and Wonder include a focus on RF along with parenting education. Increasingly, parenting programs are focusing on the importance of RF. I have developed a program called ATTACH (abbreviated from Attachment and Child Health) that is designed to help mothers of preschoolers improve their RF. It involves ten to twelve sessions with a trained facilitator and has already been shown to be effective in improving

- mothers' RF
- mothers' serve and return relationships with their chidren
- children's social-emotional adjustment
- children's security of attachment to their mothers.

In summary, RF is increasingly understood as underpinning how healthy serve and return relationships relate to healthy child development. Fortunately, it can be improved with help.

SCORES ON THE REFLECTIVE FUNCTION SURVEY

Low Risk (Score: 4)

If you scored 4, you are very sensitive to your own mental states, feelings, thoughts, and intentions and recognize how they affect your behaviour, as well as how others' mental states, feelings, thoughts, and intentions — and especially your children's — affect their behaviours. This ability enables you to be empathetic and even anticipate the outcomes of your own actions. You likely have good relationships with your children and other loved ones.

> Dr. Saunders reviews Michelle's results. "Well, Michelle, it doesn't seem like you *usually* have trouble with reflective functioning. However, I do wonder if your excitement over your recent engagement has left Bryden feeling a bit forgotten."
>
> Michelle nods in acknowledgement. "I can see that. I'm sorry, Bryden. Jim means a lot to me and I've been really excited at the thought of us being a family. I understand now that it's been hard on you, though. I should've done more to understand what you were going through."
>
> Dr. Saunders leads them through a discussion of their feelings, gradually pulling back as the channels between Michelle and Bryden open again. All three of them explore how Michelle had become so immersed and absorbed in her pleasure and excitement at

becoming engaged to Jim. So much so that she forgot to consider how the move that came with their marriage could affect Bryden.

Bryden says he likes Jim, but he hadn't thought that his mother marrying Jim would mean leaving Montreal, the only place he'd ever lived. He expresses anger that she hadn't taken the time to talk to him, like she used to do, about moving or how he would miss his friends. Michelle apologizes, again saying that she would make sure he stayed in touch with his friends in Montreal, and that he could go visit on long weekends and holidays. She'd already spoken to Marc's mom, who said he could visit any time.

Eventually, eyes sparkling through unfallen tears, Bryden says, "I know this is a big deal. And I shouldn't have run away." Leaning toward him, Michelle can't help but enfold her lanky, loveable adolescent in her arms. After a moment, Bryden says, "Love you, Mom." Soon they are laughing and goofing around together — just like always.

Moderate Risk (Score: 1–3)

Sometimes you are reflective and sometimes you are not. Do not be alarmed if you fall into this category, as the majority of parents do as well. The good news is that evidence suggests RF is a learned skill that can be improved by practising it. Take a few minutes to simply reflect on how you are feeling at the moment. What thoughts have been going through your head? How do you react to those thoughts? Next, take a look at others around you and try to guess what they are thinking and how they might feel. This may prove challenging at first, since most of these thoughts typically occur unconsciously. But the more you practise, the more second nature it will become.

Reflective function is a skill that affects how we interact with everyone, but it is especially important to develop strong RF with your child. At the end of each day, take a few minutes to review your children's actions. Pick out one or two particular behaviours and try to imagine what they were thinking or feeling to inspire the behaviour. These can be mundane behaviours, like your twelve-year-old son coming to you to ask if he can go to a friend's after dinner, or something more noticeable, like your six-year-old child repeatedly ignoring your requests to pick up her toys, or your one-year-old throwing his food on the floor. What do you think prompted these behaviours? What might be their underlying mental state, feelings, thoughts, or intentions?

If your child is old enough, talk with them about your reflections and see if you were right. These talks might make you a little uncomfortable at first, especially if you are not the sort of person inclined to discuss feelings, but you may be surprised by how much your children will benefit from your apparent care and concern. Do this with your partner and friends, too. You will find they appreciate that you care enough to ask whether you accurately guessed their thoughts and feelings motivating their behaviour. Perhaps most importantly, do this with yourself. Why do you think you acted in certain ways over the day? What were you feeling? Name your emotions. What were you thinking? This is not about changing your emotions or reactions, but simply getting in touch with them, enabling you to gain insight.

As well, check with your family physician, nurse practitioner, or public health nurse about parenting programs in your community that contain elements of RF training. A good example is Circle of Security, a series of parent group training sessions designed to teach parents to better read their children's emotions and support their emotional development. While Circle of Security programs are most relevant to parents of younger children, they provide lessons that can be useful for parenting children of any age. Search online for resources and programs in your community that offer parenting resources using terms such as *parenting support* or *parenting classes* and the name of your town/city/region. Programs directly related to reflective function may be found by using the search term *mindfulness parenting*. Books are also available on the topic, such as *The Mindful Parent* by Charlotte Peterson, *Mindful Parenting* by Kristen Race, or *Parenting from the Inside Out* by Daniel Siegel and Mary Hartzell. Also, many websites offer great online resources, such as Mindful Families (www.mindfulfamilies.ca).

Dr. Saunders flips through her notes, realizing that this was a risk for both Michelle and Bryden. While sometimes they got along well, other times they totally missed what the other was feeling or thinking, and this is exactly where they got into trouble. This was how Bryden ended up alone in Montreal.

"Well, I can certainly see you two care about each other. But I have noticed some issues that might be affecting how you get along. For instance, Bryden, why don't you tell us a little about your experiences going to school."

Michelle wonders where this is going. School's certainly not the problem here. Bryden loves school. He has never faked sick or needed prodding out the door, the way she had as a child. So it's with a bit of shock that she registers the first words Bryden says.

"It was awful," he says. "It's always been awful."

"Bryden!" Michelle cries. "How can you say that? You do so well in school. And you have so many friends!"

"No thanks to you," grumbles Bryden. "Every time I figure stuff out we move."

Michelle bites her lip. They had moved around a bit over the years — three times in six years, if she allows herself an honest tally. But that had all been for him, not for her.

Bryden voices that she never thought of him when they kept moving when he was in elementary and junior high school. All those times he had to start at a new school *again*. He had to make new friends *again*. He had to learn the ropes in the neighbourhood *again*.

"I … I never knew it was so hard for you. You never complained. And I wanted to be close to work whenever my job changed, so we could spend more time together. I didn't want you to grow up a latchkey kid like I was."

"I don't care about letting myself in after school. I care about my friends."

Michelle paused, tears in her eyes, saying, "I … I … didn't realize. I was thinking that it was better for me to reduce my commute to work so I would be home sooner after school and to see you at lunch time. Since it was just us, I didn't want you to be alone. I didn't think of how the changes would affect you. I thought I was doing the right thing."

"Well, you weren't!" he shot back.

Michelle recoils and says, "It was for your own good, but you don't get it!"

The psychologist asks them to pause and talk about how this conversation with the back and forth accusations was making them both feel. "How do you think it's making Bryden feel? Michelle feel?" She takes some time to explain the value of trying to understand each other's thoughts and feelings and how they relate to behaviour.

For instance, she asks, "Do you think that your mother had a hard time as a latchkey kid, like she said? That means she came home to an empty house when she was little, using the key to let herself in. How do you think her feelings about that influenced her actions in moving to be close to your school each time she changed jobs?" The psychologist could see the light come on for Bryden when they discuss this angle.

Soon after, Michelle, now calm, can understand why the move to Toronto was so frightening for Bryden and why Bryden's friends mean so much to him. Together they began discussing a plan for allowing Bryden to maintain his current friendships while supporting their transition to life in Toronto. They also agreed to keep talking and to try harder to understand and be considerate of each other. They had the summer to figure it all out, but they were confident that they could.

High Risk (Score: 0)

First, this test is not one hundred percent accurate, as suggested in the introduction of this book. However, if you scored 0 and you are concerned, I recommend you reach out first to your family physician or nurse practitioner for advice. Ask them if they are aware of, or can recommend, a professional expert or clinic with a focus on in infant–parent or child–parent psychotherapy. Alternatively, ask them if they can recommend an expert in parent–infant or parent–child interaction guidance. A developmental pediatrician, psychologist, nurse specialist, or social worker may possess this expertise. If they are unable to suggest someone, search out resources in your community using the online search terms *child development clinic, child development services*, or *developmental pediatrician* to see what you can find.

Be sure to refer to the tips above under Moderate Risk. It is also possible that you have experiences of trauma or other risk factors that require more help, so review the other chapters that are relevant. Hopefully some of your scores from the other chapter surveys will help you figure out what kind of help you need. Psychological or psychiatric help may be helpful, as well as family therapy, if your low RF is impacting your relationships with your family. For books on infant–parent psychotherapy or child–parent psychotherapy geared towards a general audience, I recommend *Raising an Emotionally Intelligent Child* by John Gottman. For helping you to understand how your own trauma history (see chapter 1) may be impacting your ability to be reflective in your relationships, I recommend *Adult Children of Emotionally Immature Parents: How to Heal from Distant, Rejecting, or Self-Involved Parents* by Lindsay Gibson.

Dr. Saunders reviews her notes a final time. Her face retains its well-honed neutrality, but inside she senses profound conflict between her patients. She sets the notebook aside and leans forward, hands on her knees.

"Michelle, I think it might be best if we make a little time after this appointment to talk, just the two of us."

Michelle agrees, and at their next appointment she begins by going over her childhood. The youngest of four, her mother suffered from clinical depression and was often unavailable.

"She was in the nuthouse most of the time," Michelle explains. She died when I was sixteen. We say it was a car accident, though we're not sure how accidental it was. Dad worked a lot to make sure he could afford the mortgage and put food on the table.

He was an okay guy, but I didn't really know him much. He used to say my older sisters raised me, but mostly I raised myself, really."

Michelle got pregnant in high school. The boyfriend split, which left her alone. She chose to bring the baby to term and put her up for adoption.

"That must have been extremely upsetting for you," Dr. Saunders says.

Michelle shrugs. "I guess. It's hard to remember much. I started partying pretty hard around then."

The years blur together and Michelle can't say much about what happened or when, until she turned twenty-three. She got pregnant again, with Bryden, and this time she decided to keep it. "But not the guy," she adds with a smile. "I got clean and stayed clean. Fourteen years last month. It wasn't always easy. I worked hard at the office and harder at home. But every night Bryden ate, had a roof over his head, and had me to tuck him in. Every single night."

The moves — and there were several, she admits — were always because of work. Shorter hours, better pay — it all translated into more for Bryden, and that was the only factor that mattered.

"And how did Bryden respond to those moves?"

Another shrug. "Kids adapt. They make new friends. All those childhood buddies just fade away eventually anyway. It's the mother that matters. A kid needs a mother. And I was there. Every second I could be, I was there. Plus, he hugged me all the time and told me

he loved me. No one else ever did that. Not until Jim."
She tweaks the diamond ring on her finger, ensuring
the gem is prominently displayed.

"But clearly this latest move has upset him. Tell me,
how did you first discuss the move to Toronto with him?"

"We didn't 'discuss' anything. Jim's job is in Toronto.
Jim proposed. His job's way better than mine, and I
can transfer to a Toronto branch anyway. Bryden is too
young to bum around Montreal on his own, and anyway he belongs with his mother."

"So when he ran away to Montreal, that was the
first objection, for lack of a better term, that he'd raised?"

"I dunno. I guess. He whines sometimes, but what
kid doesn't? He'd always been reasonable before. I
have no idea where this selfishness is coming from."

"Could it be shock?"

"Shock at a bigger house in a nicer neighbourhood?
Shock at seeing his mother happy? Is that supposed to
be hard to adjust to? No, I don't know what's gotten
into him. He won't be going to Montreal ever again
with this attitude, I can tell you that much."

"What about his friends?"

"Clearly they're a bad influence. Where else is this
behaviour coming from?" She adds, "He is just so self-
ish! Sometimes I think he is trying to ruin my life!"

Dr. Saunders jots down several notes. This visit, she
thinks, will be the first of many.

Chapter 8

Social Support and Co-Parenting

Parents need all the help they can get.
The strongest as well as the most fragile
family requires a vital network of social
supports.

— Bernice Weissbourd

Suzanne gives baby Charlotte a final once-over,
checking for bits of exposed skin that might get a nip
of the winter chill, and lifts the car seat from the back
of her SUV. Charlotte barely stirs as Suzanne totters
beneath the weight of the car seat, shifting the handle
to achieve a more bearable grip. She grabs the diaper bag with her other hand, struggles to close the
straps over the crescent-shaped breastfeeding pillow
bulging from it, and staggers to the door of the clinic.

It's just a few steps away but the cold is bitter and a sheath of ice has settled over every flat surface.

A mother with a stroller holds the door for Suzanne as she approaches. Suzanne gives her a nod of thanks and sidles inside, where a dozen mothers and a few fathers mingle in a small reception area. Children not quite old enough for school mill about their parents' legs or play with the toys in the far corner of the room, but most of the children Suzanne sees are Charlotte's age and too young for much beyond peekaboo.

Two public health nurses enter and begin circling about the room, chatting with parents and waving at the children. This is Suzanne's first parenting group, but clearly the same can't be said for most of these mothers. Watching their animated faces and hearing their friendly voices and occasional laughter makes her feel better about lugging Charlotte out in this miserable weather. Soon everyone is settled and one of the public health nurses signals everyone's attention.

"Excuse me! Hi, everyone. Thanks so much for braving the cold and coming out today. We've got a very special guest for you this morning. Dr. Morris is a researcher from the university who focuses on neuroscience and early child development. She's also a nurse. Please give her a big hand."

Suzanne applauds along with the others as a tall, curly-haired woman takes the podium. "Thank you very much. I'd like to talk to you today about the importance of social support."

Dr. Morris explains several concepts that are new

to Suzanne's ears: toxic stress, serve and return relationships, resilience. Suzanne listens closely, thankful that Charlotte is having no trouble sleeping today, allowing her to concentrate. Dr. Morris explains how toxic stress can affect children's development in all sorts of ways, but how a strong parent–child relationship can counteract it. And how the quality of your social support network can, in turn, improve your ability to forge a strong parent–child relationship.

"This week I thought it would be good to evaluate your level of social support." As Dr. Morris speaks, the two public health nurses start handing out questionnaires and pens. "You don't need to share your results with anyone if you don't want to, and I encourage you not to ask other people to share theirs. This is just for you, and I don't want to make anyone uncomfortable. But your two nurses and I are very happy to talk to you afterward if you have any concerns."

The public health nurses nod and smile as the parents busy themselves in filling out the questionnaires. Suzanne takes one with a smile and begins scanning the first page.

THE SOCIAL SUPPORT SURVEY

The following survey is often given to parents in research settings to assess the amount of social support they have available to them. Take the survey now and then see the end of the chapter for your results and recommended resources.

Social Support Survey

1. There is a special person who is around when I am in need.

	Very strongly disagree	Strongly disagree	Mildly disagree	Neutral	Mildly agree	Strongly agree	Very strongly agree
SCORE	1	2	3	4	5	6	7

2. There is a special person with whom I can share my joys and sorrows.

	Very strongly disagree	Strongly disagree	Mildly disagree	Neutral	Mildly agree	Strongly agree	Very strongly agree
SCORE	1	2	3	4	5	6	7

3. I have a special person who is a real source of comfort to me.

	Very strongly disagree	Strongly disagree	Mildly disagree	Neutral	Mildly agree	Strongly agree	Very strongly agree
SCORE	1	2	3	4	5	6	7

4. There is a special person in my life who cares about my feelings.

	Very strongly disagree	Strongly disagree	Mildly disagree	Neutral	Mildly agree	Strongly agree	Very strongly agree
SCORE	1	2	3	4	5	6	7

5. My family really tries to help me.

	Very strongly disagree	Strongly disagree	Mildly disagree	Neutral	Mildly agree	Strongly agree	Very strongly agree
SCORE	1	2	3	4	5	6	7

6. I get the emotional help and support I need from my family.

Very strongly disagree	Strongly disagree	Mildly disagree	Neutral	Mildly agree	Strongly agree	Very strongly agree
1	2	3	4	5	6	7

SCORE

7. I can talk about my problems with my family.

Very strongly disagree	Strongly disagree	Mildly disagree	Neutral	Mildly agree	Strongly agree	Very strongly agree
1	2	3	4	5	6	7

SCORE

8. My family is willing to help me make decisions.

Very strongly disagree	Strongly disagree	Mildly disagree	Neutral	Mildly agree	Strongly agree	Very strongly agree
1	2	3	4	5	6	7

SCORE

9. My friends really try to help me.

Very strongly disagree	Strongly disagree	Mildly disagree	Neutral	Mildly agree	Strongly agree	Very strongly agree
1	2	3	4	5	6	7

SCORE

10. I can count on my friends when things go wrong.

Very strongly disagree	Strongly disagree	Mildly disagree	Neutral	Mildly agree	Strongly agree	Very strongly agree
1	2	3	4	5	6	7

SCORE

11. I have friends with whom I can share my joys and sorrows.

Very strongly disagree	Strongly disagree	Mildly disagree	Neutral	Mildly agree	Strongly agree	Very strongly agree
1	2	3	4	5	6	7

SCORE

---

12. I can talk about my problems with my friends.

	Very strongly disagree	Strongly disagree	Mildly disagree	Neutral	Mildly agree	Strongly agree	Very strongly agree
SCORE	1	2	3	4	5	6	7

Tally responses in each row:

Score 61+: read *low risk*

Score 36–60: read *moderate risk*

Score 12–35: read *high risk*

SOCIAL SUPPORT IS ALL ABOUT RELATIONSHIPS

If you recall the ideas described in the Introduction, toxic stress is *only* toxic in the absence of supportive relationships. Research has shown, repeatedly and unequivocally, that social support is associated with positive outcomes in everything from birth complications to behavioural issues, diabetes to mental illness, and heart surgery recovery to cancer prognosis. My own research has shown that social support received by mothers in pregnancy and the postpartum period can even prevent skin conditions such as psoriasis in their eighteen-month-olds, potentially by lowering the toddlers' stress-hormone levels.

With respect to children's health and development, social support can act as an important buffer against the effects of toxic stress[173] caused by, for example, parental depression and addiction. Strong interpersonal relationships with parents or others in a child's social network contributes to their resilience, allowing them to succeed despite exposure to dozens of risk factors, including many discussed in previous chapters of this book.

The size and quality of a family's social network is a powerful predictor of children's health and development. In contrast, lack of social support is tightly linked to many preventable physical, social-emotional, and mental disorders. Social support is so important that it is even described as a "determinant of health."[174] That is, the quality and quantity of social support you have helps determine how healthy you are. When assessing the health of a given population, one might initially think the most direct way to do so would be to count the number of hospitals, doctors, and other health-care providers available. However, a far more effective strategy might be to count the number of social supports that citizens enjoy.

WHAT IS SOCIAL SUPPORT?

Social support is defined as interactions with family members, friends, peers, health professionals, and social workers that communicate information, esteem, practical aid, or emotional help.[175] When you are sufficiently supported, you perceive that help is available from those around you when you need it. Support can come from a range of sources beyond the ones we might suspect: teachers, a neighbourhood librarian, parents of your children's friends, or the leader of an afterschool playgroup can all act as essential pillars of social support.

Social support is typically thought of as having four key components:[176]

- *informational support,* when someone provides you with information about resources;
- *emotional support,* when others show empathy, compassion, and genuine concern for you;
- *instrumental support,* when others give you practical aid, like help with housekeeping, caring for children, offering transportation, or paying bills; and
- *affirmational support,* when others say or do things that are intended to provide encouragement, motivation, or aid. This type of support may particularly contribute to positive feeling states because it gives rise to the feeling that you are worthwhile.

Each component of social support can improve your sense of self-worth. Through the words and actions of the person providing social support, the support recipient hears, "I matter to this person." Social support is also reciprocal. People who provide social support benefit from their actions through the positive feelings they get from helping someone. This is especially true when the person can recall receiving social support themselves, which makes the concept of "giving back" essential to the sustainability of social support as a positive social force. Parents must also fill a socially supportive role for their children in order to provide a healthy environment for their development.

SOCIAL SUPPORT AND CO-PARENTING

More broadly, social support can be thought of as a key element of successful relationships between parents. Parents in intimate relationships who support each other well tend to sustain each other — they have the energy and resources required to parent their children well. It has been long established that satisfying marital relationships are associated with greater parental well-being, more positive parental attitudes towards children and the parenting role, greater involvement with infants and sensitivity to them (that is, healthy serve and return relationships), an increased sense of competence in the ability to care for children, and more optimal child development. This suggests that in situations of marital conflict, the stress parents face can trickle down to affect children's health and development. Recent research shows that couples therapy can directly benefit children's adjustment and improve parenting by facilitating greater social support between partners.[177]

Social support is also important whether or not people are in intimate or romantic relationships. Typically, two people who have committed to parent a given child or children, outside of the traditional mother–father married family structure, are considered "co-parents." Mutually supportive co-parents are more likely to engage in healthy serve and return relationships with their children, supporting their development.[178-79]

Co-parenting can come in many forms, including people in parenting roles who may be friends or grandparents, or in other types of relationships, including lesbian, gay, or transgendered ones. Research repeatedly demonstrates that it is not *family structure* (for example, two-parent versus one-parent families, traditional versus non-traditional families) that is important for children's health and development, but rather *family processes*, defined as the quality of supportive parenting and family relationships, that are most important.[180]

Partners and co-parents who support each other even reduce the risk of child abuse across generations.[181] Parents who were subject to harsh and abusive parenting as children are at greater risk for treating their own children harshly. However, if the parent is linked romantically to a partner who offers warmth and positive communication, the risk that he or she will engage in abusive parenting greatly diminishes.

HOW DOES SOCIAL SUPPORT WORK?

Inadequate social support is correlated with smaller social networks and fewer close relationships, factors that increase the risk for poor mental health. In contrast, adequate social support increases a person's sense of purpose, belonging, and self-worth, which may benefit mental health, increase motivation for self-care, help prevent a minor problem from progressing into a more serious one, and modulate the neuroendocrine (hypothalamic-pituitary-adrenal axis) response to stress.[182]

The perceived availability of social support in the face of a stressful event may lead to a more benign appraisal of the situation, thereby preventing a cascade of negative emotional, behavioural, and neuroendocrine responses. Thus, it is not only *receiving* social support that is important, but the *perception* that it is available if needed that can reduce the negative emotional impact of a stressful life event or dampen the overall response to a stressful event.

Being part of a broader social structure, including involvement in social networks at work and school or other personal connections and close relationships, increases the chance of finding various forms of support, which in turn protects against distress.[183] In other words, social support takes the toxicity out of stress and can turn stressors into tolerable or even positive stressors. Support behaviours that promote emotional and mental health include

- listening to someone's concerns;
- providing reassurance and encouragement;
- expressing understanding, concern, and trust;
- offering companionship, especially in stressful situations;
- offering care over time; and
- offering unconditional access to support.

Support behaviours that promote problem solving include

- talking;
- providing clarification, suggestions, direction;
- providing information about the source of stress from personal experience or expert knowledge

(for example, from personal experience with depression);
- referring to another resource that could help;
- monitoring, suggesting, and modelling;
- suggesting distracting activities (for example, outings or hobbies); and
- giving direct help (for example, basic needs, transportation).

Peer support from other parents is an important component of social support. Support provided by people who have experienced a similar health problem or stressor has been shown to have a positive effect on psychological well-being.[184] For example, new parents struggling to cope with life changes can often benefit from joint learning and peer support.[185]

My own research provides a compelling example of the power of social support. My team and I examined the effect of peer support for mothers with postpartum depression. In the program, called MOMS (Mothers Offering Mentorship and Support), we paired mothers who were suffering from postpartum depression with mothers who had dealt with the same issues in the past and recovered. The support providers were trained to offer social support over the telephone. Our results were compelling: Mothers experienced recovery from their symptoms in as few as four phone calls, and most mothers only required six or seven telephone calls in total. Further, in an additional and heartening finding, many of the mothers who benefited from the service promptly enrolled as support providers. They wanted to reciprocate.

The power of peers as a social support is that they offer proof that the problems you are facing can be overcome, offering, in a word, hope. Mothers in our research often spoke about the peer mentor as being the so-called light at the end of the tunnel. In summary, social support benefits parents and, moreover, is perhaps the most important predictor of children's health and development because it literally makes toxic stressors tolerable or even positive.

SCORES ON THE SOCIAL SUPPORT SURVEY

Low Risk (Score: 61 or More)

If you scored in this range, you likely have social support from friends, family, and your significant other. The support you attain from family — or that you know you can rely on — likely gives you the mental and physical energy to parent your child or children well, in ways that promote their healthy development, setting them up for lifelong success.

> Suzanne does a quick tally of her score. She got seventy-six, well within the low-risk category. She smiles. It doesn't come as much of a surprise. Mark, her husband, is always there for her, her in-laws are great, and she's got plenty of friends she still sees regularly, even if Charlotte makes movie nights a little tougher to plan these days.

Moderate Risk (Score: 36–60)

If you scored in this range, you have some good sources of social support but could benefit from more. Have a closer look at the questionnaire. In which category did you score the lowest? Was it with respect to family, friends, or your significant other? Try and gain some insight into where you could bolster your resources.

If you simply need to find more opportunities for meaningful interactions with people who could become part of your social network, many people find connections in the online community. You may also find support through mutual interests. Do you like to paint, do pottery, play a sport, read certain kinds of books, or want to learn and practise a language? Search online for groups that cater to your interests and see if a local group exists. The Meetup community (www.meetup.com) is an online and real-world network that links people with similar interests. To attain the social support we all need, we need to get out there and make it happen. So get out there!

For more specific needs, figure out where your support needs lie. Are they in the areas of parenting (serve and return), or do you need help with a mental health issue like depression? Refer to the relevant chapters in this book for suggestions on searching for resources or groups online or in your community that you can connect with to enlarge your social network and that offer opportunities for reciprocity. Also see the other chapters for suggestions on the various types of support you may need. Be sure to talk to your family physician, nurse practitioner, or public health nurse as well and ask them if they can suggest some resources in your community. You may also find more ideas below under High Risk.

Suzanne checks her tally. Fifty-six. She looks back over the categories and is not surprised to note that, while her scores for the family and friends questions were high, her relationship with Mark needs work.

They'd only been dating for six months when Suzanne got pregnant with Charlotte. Mark told her he wanted to do the right thing and, to his credit, he did. He supported her financially through the pregnancy and covers her rent and car payments now that Charlotte has been born, allowing her the maternity leave she never would have managed otherwise, since her freelance work didn't come with benefits.

That was all well and good, but the issue was he still hadn't moved in with her. He kept his own apartment across town where he spent most nights during the week. It was closer to his work, which was convenient for him, but he also admitted it allowed him to get solid sleep through the night. Part of her fumed at his selfishness — Why should she handle every midnight feeding? Why couldn't she get a decent night's sleep for once? — while the other felt a twinge of guilt. He was still working full-time, after all. Wasn't it important that he got a full night's sleep in order to do his job? These two feelings fought constantly inside her, their furor building whenever she asks him again about them getting a house. "Soon," he says. "The market's really nuts now," or "It's just not the right time."

Later that day and all through the next week, she thought about the word *undecided*. She turned the idea over in her head. She dwelled on the word. She dwelled on Mark's inability to commit to them. It was starting to get her down, especially when she was alone at night with no help and tired in the weekdays spent alone with Charlotte. During his stay with them one weekend, she was morose. But Charlotte giggled with glee when she saw him and he beamed at her with pride. *He's trying*, she thought, *but is still undecided. That's the problem*, she concluded. *I feel like I can't rely on him, and I want to. I need to be able to rely on him. That's the biggest gap in my social support.*

During the next parenting group, she flags down a nurse and asks for a recommendation for couple's counselling. The nurse discreetly takes her to a nearby office and they go over some options together. Suzanne leaves with a few cards and phone numbers. She'll have to raise the issue with Mark. It might be an uncomfortable conversation, but she trusts that he wants to make this work as much as she does.

High Risk (Score: 12–35)

If you scored in this range, you need to get creative about finding ways to bolster your support network. As suggested under Moderate Risk, go back to the questionnaire and identify the areas where your social supports are strongest and where they are weakest. While your initial reaction may be to work on the weakest areas, a better starting point may be those spheres (for example, friends, extended family) where some support already exists. You may need professional help as well, so consider talking to your family physician, nurse practitioner, or another health professional, like a counsellor. If you are unsure where to go, crisis lines, health information centres, and even simple online searches, described in more detail in the other chapters, can help you identify local resources.

In general, parents linking up with other parents can offer real advantages and opportunities. Create a parent support group and do things together like play dates and taking turns babysitting each other's children. If you are reading this book and are an expectant parent, other parents in your prenatal class are an excellent starting point. Make connections, share your contact information, and make the effort to socialize and get to know the other parents. For parents of newborns and infants, parenting support groups and centres exist in most communities and offer weekly meetings to discuss topics of relevance to parents, especially new parents. The parenting topics are often secondary to the opportunity for parents to connect with each other.

Try searching with the terms *parenting support group*, *new parents group*, or *moms group* and the name of your town/city/region to find such groups in your community. In Canada, for example, many regions have Parent Link

Centres or Parenting Resource Centres offered in conjunction with Public Health Nursing services or the YMCA and YWCA. Calling the YMCA or YWCA or searching for their websites online (along with the name of your community) may provide you with just the information you need to connect with other parents.

For parents of children from birth to five years, the Nobody's Perfect program is available in many communities (nobodysperfect.ca/home) and the nature of the support is directly tied to parents' needs and interests. For parents of children of all ages, the Triple P Parenting Program (www.triplep.net/glo-en/home) is available internationally; the website offers many resources for parents, including how to find a local provider as well as blogs from other parents.

Social support takes many shapes, and the type of support you need will vary depending on your situation. Friends, family, and other forms of informal support can provide a useful buffer against toxic stress, whereas dealing with issues such as addiction or abuse may require more formal support. Refer to the relevant chapters for details.

Suzanne shoves the questionnaire into her diaper bag, incomplete. She can't make it past the first few questions. She knows the sort of answer she's going to get and it's too painful. Fighting back tears, she waits for the earliest opportunity and slips out the door.

A few days later, Charlotte is napping and Suzanne takes the free moment to clean out the diaper bag. She stumbles across the crumpled questionnaire. A pang of unease jabs her insides. She moves to toss the paper in the garbage, pauses, and instead finds a pen in her kitchen drawer and completes the questionnaire.

The results sting all the more for their inevitability. She'd been raising Charlotte alone since Mark walked out, so there went the partner score. Her parents will very begrudgingly watch Charlotte now and then, but only after subjecting Suzanne to an excruciating litany of "I told you so," said a hundred different ways. Her friends were more sympathetic, but also more clueless. None of them had kids, and while they might listen to her vent on the phone now and then, they didn't seem to get how hard parenting was and weren't about to come by and help her with the laundry.

She thinks back to the parenting group. There'd been resources there, right? "Well, I need all sorts of help, so I qualify," she laughs sadly to herself. Rummaging through the diaper bag, she finds a few pamphlets stowed amongst the wipes and singles out one with the number for the public health clinic. *It's a start*, she thinks, and dials the number.

Chapter 9
Final Thoughts

Let your hopes, not your hurts, shape your future.

— Robert Schuller

Recently I was travelling by car to a meeting with a fellow registered nurse, who I will call Ellen. Ellen is great to talk to because she is engaging and funny as well as intelligent and accomplished, professionally. We laugh a lot when we are together. She has a wide social network and knows everyone who's anyone. With her sense of humour and wit, she gets a lot done in our region of the world. So I was surprised by what I learned in the course of our conversation.

I was telling her about this book and we got talking about the ACE questionnaire. She knew about this line of research and voiced her excitement about how it helps us health-care providers understand more about our patients. We agreed that for many nurses and doctors, understanding ACEs and the effect of early trauma enables us to have more empathy and understanding. She said that ACEs helped her shift her thinking from "What is wrong with you?" to "What happened to you?" regarding her patients. I agreed.

Then, as we talked some more, she disclosed something personal. I was very surprised to learn that she herself had a very high ACE score, "At least 4 or 5," she said. "But I'm resilient," she added with a smile and offered up her closed hand to fist pump.

She was clearly proud of all that she had accomplished in spite of a lot of early adversity. At first, she almost whispered her traumatic experiences to me. Then, more loudly, she listed the strengths in life that had sustained her: a loving and supportive spouse, strong support from her extended family, healthy relationships with her siblings, access to counselling for mental health issues when she was younger, and a good education that enabled her to obtain a job that kept the financial worries away.

Yes, we agreed, she was the definition of resilience. Ellen and I continued to talk and drifted to other subjects, laughing as we usually do together. But that conversation stayed with me for a long time. I realized from talking with Ellen how real all the topics in this book are, for so many people. It's not just academic, it's real life. And my conversation with Ellen reminded me that it's not so rare to find people who have succeeded, despite life's hurdles. Their supportive relationships and triumphs sustained them. Ellen and so many others like her give me unbounded hope.

HOPE FOR THE FUTURE

Ultimately this is a book about hope and about how the effects of big, traumatic life experiences can be changed or even made powerless by the little experiences in life. The big life experiences that seem impossible to overcome include violence, abuse, addictions, and mental health problems; the little, less noticeable experiences include healthy serve and return relationships, seeking to understand one another (reflective function), and social support.

The big life experiences are hard to ignore or miss. But what is exciting and hopeful is the power of the little experiences to change everything. Consider how important the day-to-day experiences of healthy serve and return relationships, and reflective and supportive interactions with people who care, are. They make the difference between a stressor being toxic or tolerable. The little experiences really are the most important in the big picture and can make a difference in the way you parent and how your child grows and develops. The little experiences are not so little when you consider how they foster resilience in both parents and children.

DO NOT OVERDO IT, BUT DO IT

As I emphasized in Chapter 2: Serve and Return Parenting and Chapter 7: Reflective Function, noticing and attending to your child's cues that signal their needs is paramount. But be careful about overdoing it, especially as they grow older. Initially, when babies are born, they are completely dependent on their parents and essentially experience the world through them. Babies require parents to help them regulate their responses to stress, for example, to help soothe them after an upset, or to be brave enough to try out a new and noisy toy. However, as children grow and mature, they need to master new skills and gain independence, so it is important to eventually back off and let them cope with stressors more and more themselves.

Of the pop culture parenting types I described in the introduction, two types are at particular risk for overdoing it. Helicopter parents, so-called because they seem to hover over their children to prevent them from experiencing failure in school, social life, or other activities, have children that may seem successful. But, as I suggested in the Introduction, scientific study has not determined if helicopter parents' children will learn to fly solo effectively. My guess is that they will be challenged in doing so, as they are seldom given the chance to practise. Adherents of attachment parenting, the pop culture spin-off from the research on secure parent–infant attachment, also advocates that infants and children be stressed as little as possible. There is little science to support either of these approaches, but common-sense suggests that neither approach is likely to help children be successful or resilient in the long run.

In my view, the key is moderation and knowing when to support your children in flying solo. Here again, noticing and paying attention is important. You can ask yourself the following:

- Is my child ready?
- Does my child need a nudge?

Parenting becomes a balancing act — it requires you to pull back at times but also to pay close attention to your child. If your child is acting out, consider what may be setting him or her off. Ask yourself the following:

- What are my child's underlying mental states, feelings, thoughts, or intentions? How might these relate to his or her behaviour?
- Is there something I can do to help?
- Do I need to change my approaches? Do others?
- Do I/we need outside help?

Parenting also requires flexibility along with self-forgiveness. In spite of all our knowledge, sometimes being an effective parent requires trial and error, based on your observations of what is going on in your child's life. Ask yourself the following:

- Do I need to intervene?
- Do I need to change something to help my child stay on track in becoming a successful adult?

If you judge yes, then you have to try different things, and this assumes that you will fail at least some of the time. I also think it is important that your children see both that you think they are worth the effort and that you keep trying to be the best parent you can be for your child, in the best and worst of circumstances.

I also ask myself a lot, "Am I being the parent my child needs me to be?" I am not always who my child needs me to be, but I know I can correct course. And, as I have said to many parents, you have many chances to do the right thing, meaning you should not beat yourself up for your perceived missteps as a parent.

THE POWER AND SOCIETAL RESPONSIBILITY OF SOCIAL SUPPORT

A final word on social support: Social support is so powerfully important to parenting and children's development that it is rightfully elevated to a societal responsibility. In my view, it is everyone's responsibility to make sure that families are supported adequately to do the important work that they do: raising healthy children who will become successful, independent adults.

While the emphasis of this book may seem to be on the main risk factors to parenting and children's development, ultimately parents' ability to overcome those risks and learn to recognize and return serves, for example, rests on the quality and quantity of social support available to them. Again, I strongly believe that it is a societal responsibility to prevent the traumas described in chapter 1. To the extent that it is possible, families under stress should be identified to prevent early childhood adversity, and supported to provide the best environments possible for children. The ability to be reflective or to engage in healthy serve and return interactions may be easy for some, but for others, formal social support from health and service providers may be essential to help attain those skills. Parents may also need formal social support to help overcome the effects of toxic stressors like depression or addictions.

I have spoken to many parents who are reluctant to reach out for social support, when they and their children could clearly benefit from it. Parenting is a hard job at the best of times, and given all we know about how social support can convert toxic stress into tolerable stress or even more benign or positive experiences, parents need to be encouraged to seek support and know that it is okay to ask for help. Our social structures on both a personal and community level need to be oriented towards parents to ensure help is there when they need it.

Reciprocity is also an important feature of social support. There are many opportunities for parents to "give back" to other parents or community resources when they find they no longer need social support themselves. For example, when children are grown, volunteering in the community to help other parents can be very rewarding. This opportunity may be reassuring for parents who are reluctant to ask for or receive help as parents.

In my view, reciprocity in social support is what the expression "It takes a village to raise a child" really means.

I personally do not want to live in a society where parents are not routinely supported. Parents are doing perhaps the most important job of society members: raising the next generation of healthy, high-functioning citizens. Much like the view that a society's worth may be judged by how it treats its most vulnerable citizens, a society in which parents cannot comfortably ask for help and are expected to raise their children in isolation is deeply misguided. In this spirit, I recommend that parents reach out and create the village they need to raise their child. In writing this book I hope to help parents understand the unique risks they face in their parenting as well as identify and obtain the resources they need in their village to overcome those risks.

With social support as a given, the most effective parenting involves attentive sensitivity and responsiveness, especially early in life, then gradually fostering independence. Even as children become more independent, effective parents, in my view, never stop paying attention and demonstrating caring through healthy serve and return relationships that are highly reflective and supportive.

That just might be what love looks like.

Acknowledgements

I would like to thank my husband, Dean Mullin, and sons, Maxwell and Jackson, who tolerated my having to work many extra evenings and weekends on this project. This book definitely interfered with our serve and return relationships and I will make it up to you soon! I love you and appreciate all you do to inspire me every day to be better.

I also want to thank both Justin Joschko and my editors Kathryn Lane and especially Elena Radic for scouring my anecdotes and text and suggesting innumerable ways to make my writing more accessible and interesting.

I want to thank my CHILD Studies Program research team of staff and students, especially Dr. Martha Hart, Virginia Xavier, Dr. Lubna Anis, Dr. Jordana Linder, Henry Ntanda, Elena Ali, Bikram Sekhorn, Debbie Jones, Andrea Deane, Jason Novick, Ivy Chen, and Tracey Reynaud.

Finally, I want to also thank my many colleagues, especially my long-term and most valued mentor Dr. Miriam Stewart, as well as Dr. Penny Tryphonopoulos, Dr. Linda Duffett-Leger, Dr. Gerald Giesbrecht, Dr. Tavis Campbell, Dr. Deborah Dewey, Dr. Anita Kozyrskyj, Dr. Cindy-Lee Dennis, Dr. Brent Scott, Dr. Karen Benzies, Dr. Suzanne Tough, Dr. Bonnie Kaplan, Dr. Brenda Leung, Dr. Catherine Lebel, Dr. Catherine Field, Dr. Rhonda Bell, Dr. Doug Willms, Dr. Michael Kobor, Dr. Meaghan Jones, Dr. Loretta Secco, Dr. Sarah Moore, Dr. Jason de Koning, Dr. Cheryl Gibson, and Dr. Dianne Tapp. I also want to thank my community research colleagues, Carlene Donnelly and everyone at CUPS, Joy Johnson-Green and everyone at Sonshine women's shelter, Monique Auffrey and everyone at Discovery House, so many friends at the New Brunswick Department of Health, and finally, Jim Murphy of Sykes Telecare. I also want to thank my funders, especially Saifa Koonar of the Alberta Children's Hospital Foundation, Nancy Mannix and Michelle Gagnon of the Palix Foundation, Agnes Cooke, Margaret Newell, the Prairieaction Foundation, Canada Research Chairs, Canadian Institutes of Health Research, Social Sciences and Humanities Research Council, NCE AllerGen, NCE NeuroDevNet (now Kids Brain Health), Alberta Centre for Child and Family Health Research (now PolicyWise), the Harvard Frontiers of Innovation, and an anonymous donor. Also great friends who encouraged me deserve thanks including Susan Taylor, Chris Bryant, Lisa Ploude-Bennett, Tracy King, and Kerrie Dirk. Without the support of my colleagues and funders, much of my research on the topics in this book, which both informed and inspired my thinking, could not have been completed.

Notes

1. Zucchi FC, Yao Y, Ward ID, et al. Maternal stress induces epigenetic signatures of psychiatric and neurological diseases in the offspring. 2013.

2. Babenko O, Kovalchuk I, Metz GA. Stress-induced perinatal and transgenerational epigenetic programming of brain development and mental health. *Neuroscience and Biobehavioral Reviews.* 2015;48:70–91.

3. Ellis B, Boyce T. Biological sensitivity to context. *Current Directions in Psychological Science.* 2008;17(3):183–87.

4. Mullen PE, Martin JL, Anderson JC, Romans SE, Herbison GP. The long-term impact of the physical, emotional, and sexual abuse of children: A community study. *Child Abuse and Neglect.* 1996;20(1):7–21.

5. Hillis SD, Anda RF, Dube SR, Felitti VJ, Marchbanks PA, Marks JS. The association between adverse childhood experiences and adolescent pregnancy, long-term psychosocial consequences, and fetal death. *Pediatrics.* 2004;113(2):320–27.

6. Anda RF, Whitfield CL, Felitti VJ, et al. Adverse childhood experiences, alcoholic parents, and later risk of alcoholism and depression. *Psychiatric Services.* 2002;53(8):1001–09.

7. Dube SR, Miller JW, Brown DW, et al. Adverse childhood experiences and the association with ever using alcohol and initiating alcohol use during adolescence. *Journal of Adolescent Health.* 2006;38(4):444. e441–44. e410.

8. Cunningham TJ, Ford ES, Croft JB, Merrick MT, Rolle IV, Giles WH. Sex-specific relationships between adverse childhood experiences and chronic obstructive pulmonary disease in five states. *International Journal of Chronic Obstructive Pulmonary Disease.* 2014;9:1033.

9. Dong M, Giles WH, Felitti VJ, et al. Insights into causal pathways for ischemic heart disease. *Circulation.* 2004;110(13):1761–66.

10. McDonald S, Tough S. *Alberta Adverse Childhood Experiences Survey 2013 Report.* Calgary, AB: Alberta Centre for Child, Family and Community Services;2014.

11. Kessler RC. Epidemiology of women and depression. *Journal of Affective Disorders.* 2003;74(1):5–13.

12. Thompson MP, Kingree JB, Desai S. Gender differences in long-term health consequences of physical abuse of children: Data from a nationally representative survey. *American Journal of Public Health.* 2004;94(4):599–604.

13. Hill J, Pickles A, Burnside E, et al. Child sexual abuse, poor parental care and adult depression: Evidence for different mechanisms. *British Journal of Psychiatry.* 2001;179(2):104–09.

14. Ferguson KS, Dacey CM. Anxiety, depression, and dissociation in women health care providers reporting a history of childhood psychological abuse. *Child Abuse and Neglect.* 1997;21(10):941–52.

15. Nikulina V, Widom CS, Czaja S. The role of childhood neglect and childhood poverty in predicting mental health, academic achievement and crime in adulthood. *American Journal of Community Psychology.* 2011;48(3–4):309–21.

16. Edwards VJ, Holden GW, Felitti VJ, Anda RF. Relationship between multiple forms of childhood maltreatment and adult mental health in community respondents: results from the adverse childhood experiences study. *American Journal of Psychiatry.* 2003;160(8):1453–60.

17. Wells S, Tremblay P, Flynn A, et al. Associations of hair cortisol with self-reported measures of stress and mental-health related factors in a pooled database of diverse community samples. *Stress.* 2014;17(4):334–42.

18. Chapman DP, Whitfield CL, Felitti VJ, Dube SR, Edwards VJ, Anda RF. Adverse childhood

experiences and the risk of depressive disorders in adulthood. *Journal of affective disorders.* 2004;82(2):217-225.

19. Dube S, Anda R, Felitti V, Chapman B, Williamson D, Giles W. Childhood abuse, household dysfunction and the risk of attempted suicide throughout the life span: Findings from the Adverse Childhood Experiences Study. *JAMA.* 2008;286(24):3089–96.

20. Chung EK, Nurmohamed L, Mathew L, Elo IT, Coyne JC, Culhane JF. Risky health behaviors among mothers-to-be: The impact of adverse childhood experiences. *Academic Pediatrics.* 2010;10(4):245–51.

21. Chung EK, Mathew L, Elo IT, Coyne JC, Culhane JF. Depressive symptoms in disadvantaged women receiving prenatal care: The influence of adverse and positive childhood experiences. *Ambulatory Pediatrics.* 2008;8(2):109–16.

22. Murphy A, Steele M, Dube SR, et al. Adverse childhood experiences (ACEs) questionnaire and adult attachment interview (AAI): Implications for parent-child relationships. *Child Abuse and Neglect.* 2014;38(2):224–33.

23. Montalvo-Liendo N, Fredland N, McFarlane J, Lui F, Koci AF, Nava A. The intersection of partner violence and adverse childhood experiences: Implications for research and clinical practice. *Issues in Mental Health Nursing.* 2015;36(12):989–1006.

24. McFarlane J, Symes L, Binder BK, Maddoux J, Paulson R. Maternal-child dyads of functioning: The

intergenerational impact of violence against women on children. *Maternal and Child Health Journal.* 2014;18(9):2236–43.

25. Moog NK, Entringer S, Rasmussen JM, et al. Intergenerational effect of maternal exposure to childhood maltreatment on newborn brain anatomy. *Biological Psychiatry.* 2017.

26. McDonnell CG, Valentino K. Intergenerational effects of childhood trauma: Evaluating pathways among maternal ACEs, perinatal depressive symptoms, and infant outcomes. *Child Maltreatment.* 2016;21(4):317–26.

27. Madigan S, Wade M, Plamondon A, Maguire JL, Jenkins JM. Maternal adverse childhood experience and infant health: Biomedical and psychosocial risks as intermediary mechanisms. *J Pediatr.* 2017;1:1–9.

28. Fredland N, McFarlane J, Symes L, Maddoux J. Exploring the association of maternal adverse childhood experiences with maternal health and child behavior following intimate partner violence. *Journal of Women's Health.* 2017.

29. Mangham C, McGrath P, Reid G, Stewart M. Resiliency: Relevance to heath problems: Detailed Analysis. Halifax, NS: Atlantic Health Promotion Research Centre, Dalhousie University; 1994.

30. Ainsworth M, Blehar M, Waters B, Wall S. *Patterns of attachment: A Psychological Study of the Strange Situation.* Hillsdale, NJ: Lawrence Erlbaum Associates; 1978.

31. Groh AM, Fearon RP, Bakermans-Kranenburg MJ, Van IJzendoorn MH, Steele RD, Roisman GI. The significance of attachment security for children's social competence with peers: A meta-analytic study. *Attachment and Human Development.* 2014;16(2):103–36.

32. Hoeve M, Stams G, van der Put C, Dubas J, van der Laan P, Gerris J. A meta-analysis of attachment to parents and delinquency. *Journal of Abnormal Child Psychology.* 2012;40(5):771–85.

33. Colonnesi C, Draijer E, Stams J, Van der Bruggen C, Bogels S, Noom M. The relation between insecure attachment and child anxiety: A meta-analytic review. *Journal of Clinical Child and Adolescent Psychology.* 2011;40(4):630–45.

34. van IJzendoorn M, Dijkstra J, Bus A. Attachment, intelligence and language: A meta-analysis. *Social Development.* 1995;4(2):115–28.

35. Puig J, Englund MM, Simpson JA, Collins WA. Predicting adult physical illness from infant attachment: A prospective longitudinal study. *Health Psychology.* 2013;32(4):409.

36. Masten AS. *Ordinary magic: Resilience in development.* Guilford Publications; 2015.

37. Barnard K, Guralnick MJ. Influencing parent-child interactions for children at risk. *The effectiveness of Early Interventions.* Toronto, ON: Paul Brooks; 1997:99–126.

38. NCAST. *Keys to Caregiving.* Seattle, WA: NCAST Programs; 1999.

39. Pagani L, Boulerice B, Vitaro F, Tremblay RE. Effects of poverty on academic failure and delinquency in boys: A change and process model approach. *Journal of Child Psychology and Psychiatry and Allied Disciplines.* 1999;40(8):1209–19.

40. Meier MH, Slutske WS, Arndt S, Cadoret RJ. Impulsive and callous traits are more strongly associated with delinquent behavior in higher risk neighborhoods among boys and girls. *Journal of Abnormal Psychology.* 2008;117(2):377.

41. Crittenden P. *Raising parents: Attachment, parenting and child safety.* London, UK: Willan; 2008.

42. Federal/Provincial/Territorial Advisory Committee on Population Health and Health Security. *Building an early childhood development system utilizing a population health perspective.* Ottawa, ON: Health Canada;2003.

43. Ludy-Dobson C, Perry B. The role of healthy relational interactions in buffering the impact of childhood trauma. *Working with children to heal interpersonal trauma: The power of play.* 2010:26–43.

44. Keating D, Hertzman C. *Developmental health and the wealth of nations: Social, biological, and educational dynamics.* New York, NY: Guilford Press; 1999.

45. Hair NL, Hanson JL, Wolfe BL, Pollak SD. Association of child poverty, brain development, and academic achievement. *JAMA Pediatrics.* 2015;169(9):822–29.

46. McLoyd V, Shanahan M. Poverty, parenting, and children's mental health. *American Sociological Review.* 1993;58:351–66.

47. Becker G. *A treatise on the family.* Boston, MA: Harvard University Press; 1991.

48. McLoyd V, Wilson L. Maternal behavior, social support, and economic conditions as predictors of distress in children. *New Directions for Child Development.* Winter 1990(46):49–69.

49. McMahon RJ, Peters RD, eds. *The effects of parental dysfunction on children.* New York, NY: Kluwer Academic/Plenum Publishers;2002.

50. Elder G, Conger K, Foster E, Ardelt M. Families under economic presssure. *Journal of Family Issues.* 1992;13(1):5–37.

51. Kalil A, DeLeire T. *Family investments in children's potential.* Mahwah, NJ: Lawrence Erlbaum Associates; 2004.

52. Olds D, Kitzman H, Hanks C, et al. Effects of nurse home visiting on maternal and child functioning: Age-9 follow-up of a randomized trial. *Pediatrics.* 2007;120(4):832–45.

53. Dougherty G. Ensuring the best start in life: Targeting versus universality in early child development. *IRPP Choices.* 2007;13(8).

54. Bose J, Hedden S, Lipari R, Park-Lee E, Porter J, Pemberton M. *Key substance use and mental health indicators in the United States: Results from the 2015 National Survey on Drug Use and Health.* Center for Behavioral Health Statistics and Quality; 2016.

55. Solomon DA, Keller MB, Leon AC, et al. Multiple recurrences of major depressive disorder. *American Journal of Psychiatry.* 2000;157(2):229–33.

56. Yim IS, Tanner Stapleton LR, Guardino CM, Hahn-Holbrook J, Dunkel Schetter C. Biological and psychosocial predictors of postpartum depression: Systematic review and call for integration. *Annual Review of Clinical Psychology.* 2015;11:99–137.

57. De Moor M, Beem A, Stubbe J, Boomsma D, De Geus E. Regular exercise, anxiety, depression and personality: A population-based study. *Preventive Medicine.* 2006;42(4):273–79.

58. Letourneau NL, Duffett-Leger L, Stewart M, et al. Canadian mothers' perceived support needs during postpartum depression. *Journal of Obstetric, Gynecologic and Neonatal Nursing.* 2007;36(5):441-449.

59. Morse CA, Buist A, Durkin S. First-time parenthood: Influences on pre- and postnatal adjustment in fathers and mothers. *Journal of Psychosomatic Obstetrics & Gynecology.* 2001;21(2):109–20.

60. Kim P, Swain JE. Sad dads: Paternal pospartum depression. *Psychiatry.* 2007;4(2):36–47.

61. O'Hara MW, Swain AM. Rates and risk of postpartum depression: A meta-analysis. *International Review of Psychiatry.* 1996;8(1):37.

62. Paulson J, Bazemore S. Prenatal and postpartum depression in fathers and its association with maternal depression: A meta-analysis. *JAMA.* 2010;19:1961–69.

63. Letourneau NL, Dennis C-L, Benzies K, et al. Postpartum depression is a family affair: Addressing

the impact on mothers, fathers, and children. *Issues in Mental Health Nursing.* 2012;33(7):445–57.

64. Doucet S. Postpartum depression and postpartum psychosis: Differentiation and clinical implications. *JOGNN.* in press.

65. Fairbrother N, Woody S. New mothers' thoughts of harm related to the newborn. *Archives of Womens Mental Health.* 2008;11:221–29.

66. Paulson JF, Bazemore SD. Prenatal and postpartum depression in fathers and its association with maternal depression: A meta-analysis. *Jama.* 2010;303(19):1961–69.

67. Gavin NI, Gaynes BN, Lohr KN, Meltzer-Brody S, Gartlehner G, Swinson T. Perinatal depression: A systematic review of prevalence and incidence. *Obstetrics and Gynecology.* 2005;106(5, Part 1):1071–83.

68. Cooper PJ, Murray L. Postnatal depression. *British Medical Journal.* 1998;316(7148):1884–86.

69. Letourneau N, Salmani M, Duffett-Leger L. Maternal depressive symptoms and parenting of children from birth to 12 years. *Western Journal of Nursing Research.* 2010;32(5):662–85.

70. Goodman JH. Paternal postpartum depression, its relationship to maternal postpartum depression, and implications for family health. *Journal of Advanced Nursing.* 2004;45(1):26–35.

71. Wee KY, Skouteris H, Pier C, Richardson B, Milgrom J. Correlates of ante- and postnatal depression in fathers: A systematic review. *Journal of Affective Disorders.* 2011;130(3):358–77.

72. Holopainen D. The experience of seeking help for postnatal depression. *Australian Journal of Advanced Nursing.* March-May 2002;19(3):39–44.

73. Leinonen JA, Solantaus TS, Punamaeki R-L. Parental mental health and children's adjustment: The quality of marital interaction and parenting as mediating factors. *Journal of Child Psychology and Psychiatry.* Feb 2003;44(2):227–41.

74. Davey SJ, Dziurawiec S, O'Brien-Malone A. Men's voices: Postnatal depression from the perspective of male partners. *Qualitative Health Research.* Feb 2006; 16(2):206–20.

75. Meignan M, Davis MW, Thomas SP, Droppleman PG. Living with postpartum depression: The father's experience. *American Journal of Maternal/Child Nursing.* 1999;24(4):202–08.

76. Kahn J, Coyne J, Margolin G. Depression and marital disagreement: The social construction of despair. *Journal of Social and Personal Relations.* 1985;2:447–61.

77. Pan HS, Neidig PH, O'Leary KD. Predicting mild and severe husband-to-wife physical aggression. *Journal of Consultative Clinical Psychology.* 1994;62(5):975–81.

78. Sayers C, Kohn C, Fresco D, Belleck A, Sarwer D. Marital cognitions and depression in the context of marital discord. *Cognitive Therapy and Research.* 2001;25(6):713–32.

79. Veríssimo M, Santos AJ, Fernandes C, Shin N, Vaughn BE. Associations between attachment

security and social competence in preschool children. *Merrill-Palmer Quarterly.* 2014;60(1):80–99.

80. West K, Matthews B, Kerns K. Mother-child attachment and cognitive perfromance in middle childhood: An examination of mediating mechanisms. *Early Childhood Research Quaterly.* 2013;28(2):259–70.

81. Letourneau NL, Hart JM, MacMaster FP. Association between nonparenting adult's attachment patterns and bain structure and function: A systematic review of neuroimaging studies. *SAGE Open Nursing.* 2017;3:2377960816685572.

82. Beck CT. Postpartum depression: A metasynthesis. *Qualitative Health Research.* 2002;12(4):453–72.

83. Hanington L, Ramchandani P, Stein A. Parental depression and child temperament: Assessing child to parent effects in a longitudinal population study. *Infant Behavior and Development.* 2010;33:88–95.

84. Kozyrskyj A, Mai X, McGrath P, HayGlass K, Becker A, MacNeil B. Continued exposure to maternal distress in early life is associated with an increased risk of childhood asthma. *American Journal of Respiratory and Critical Care Medicine.* 2008;177:142–47.

85. Brennan PA, Hammen C, Andersen MJ, Bor W, Najman JM, Williams GM. Chronicity, severity, and timing of maternal depressive symptoms: Relationships with child outcomes at age 5. *Developmental Psychology.* 2000;36(6):759–66.

86. Kingston D, Tough S. Prenatal and postnatal maternal mental health and school-age child

development: A systematic review. *Maternal and Child Health Journal.* 2014;18(7):1728–41.

87. Goodman SH, Gotlib IH. Risk for psychopathology in the children of depressed mothers: A developmental model for understanding mechanisms of transmission. *Psychological Review.* 1999;106(3):458–90.

88. Luoma I, Tamminen T, Kaukonen P, et al. Longitudinal study of maternal depressive symptoms and child well-being. *Journal of the American Academy of Child and Adolescent Psychiatry.* 2001;40(12):1367–74.

89. Cummings EM, Keller PS, Davies PT. Towards a family process model of maternal and paternal depressive symptoms: Exploring multiple relations with child and family functioning. *Journal of Child Psychology and Psychiatry.* 2005;46(5):479–89.

90. Paulson JF, Keefe HA, Leiferman JA. Early parental depression and child language development. *Journal of Child Psychology and Psychiatry.* 2009;50(3):254–62.

91. Ramchandani P, Stein A, Evans J, O'Connor TG. Paternal depression in the postnatal period and child development: A prospective population study. *Lancet.* 2005;365(9478):2201–05.

92. Elgar F, Curtis L, McGrath P, Waschbusch D, Stewart S. Antecedent-consequence conditions in maternal mood and child adjustment: A four-year cross-lagged study. *Journal of Clinical Child and Adolescent Psychiatry.* 2003;32(3):362–74.

93. Grace SL, Evindar A, Stewart DE. The effect of postpartum depression on child cognitive development and behavior: A review and critical analysis of the literature. *Archives of Women's Mental Health.* Nov 2003;6(4):263–74.

94. Kane P, Garber J. The relations among depression in fathers, children's psychopathology, and father-child conflict: A meta-analysis. *Clinical Psychology Review.* 2004;24(3):339–60.

95. Murray L, Sinclair D, Cooper P, Ducournau P, Turner P. The socioemotional development of 5-year-old children of postnatally depressed mothers. *Journal of Child Psychology and Psychiatry and Allied Disciplines.* 1999;40(8):1259–71.

96. Forman DR, O'Hara MW, Stuart S, Gorman LL, Larsen KE, Coy KC. Effective treatment for postpartum depression is not sufficient to improve the developing mother-child relationship. *Development and Psychopathology.* Spring 2007;19(2):585–602.

97. O'Hara MW, Dennis CL, McCabe JE, Galbally M. Evidence-Based Treatments and Pathways to Care. *Identifying perinatal depression and anxiety: Evidence-based practice in screening, psychosocial assessment and management.* 2015:177.

98. Letourneau N, Secco L, Colpitts J, Aldous S, Stewart M, Dennis CL. Quasi-experimental evaluation of a telephone-based peer support intervention for maternal depression. *Journal of Advanced Nursing.* 2015.

99. Arroll B, Elley C, Fishman T, et al. Antidepressants versus placebo for depresssion in primary care (Review). *Cochrane Library.* 2009;3:1–65.

100. McKay J, Shaver-Hast L, Sharnoff W, Warren M, Wright H. A family approach to treatment of postpartum depression. *Zero to Three.* 2009;29(5):35–39.

101. Walsh C, MacMillan HL, Jamieson E. The relationship between parental substance abuse and child maltreatment: Findings from the Ontario Health Supplement. *Child Abuse and Neglect.* 2003;27(12):1409–25.

102. Hall CW, Webster RE. Traumatic symptomatology characteristics of adult children of alcoholics. *Journal of Drug Education.* 2002;32(3):195–211.

103. Johnson JL, Leff M. Children of substance abusers: overview of research findings. *Pediatrics.* May 1999;103(5 Pt 2):1085–99.

104. Rangarajan S. Mediators and moderators of parental alcoholism effects on offspring self-esteem. *Alcohol and Alcoholism.* 2008;43(4):481–91.

105. Plescia-Pikus M, Long-Suter E, Wilson JP. Achievement, well-being, intelligence, and stress reaction in adult children of alcoholics. *Psychological Reports.* 1988;62(2):603–09.

106. Kearns-Bodkin JN, Leonard KE. Relationship functioning among adult children of alcoholics. *Journal of Studies on Alcohol and Drugs.* 2008;69(6):941–50.

107. Killeen T, Brady KT. Parental stress and child behavioral outcomes following substance abuse residential treatment: Follow-up at 6 and 12 months. *Journal of Substance Abuse Treatment.* 2000;19(1):23–29.

108. El-Guebaly N, Offord DR. The offspring of alcoholics: A critical review. *American Journal of Psychiatry.* 1977;134(4):357–65.

109. Jacob T, Krahn GL, Leonard K. Parent-child interactions in families with alcoholic fathers. *Journal of Consulting and Clinical Psychology.* 1991;59(1):176.

110. Dunn MG, Tarter RE, Mezzich AC, Vanyukov M, Kirisci L, Kirillova G. Origins and consequences of child neglect in substance abuse families. *Clinical Psychology Review.* 2002;22(7):1063–90.

111. World Health Organization. *Global status report on alcohol and health.* Luxembourg 2014.

112. Organization WH. Health topics: Substance abuse. 2017.

113. Hall P. Intimate violence: 2009/10 BCS. In: Smith K, ed. *Homicides, Firearm Offenses adn Intimate Violence, 2009/10: Supplementary Volume 2 to Crime in England and Wales.* Vol 2. London, UK: Home Office; 2011.

114. Watson D, Parsons S. *Domestic abuse of women and men in Ireland: Report on the National Study of Domestic Abuse.* Dublin: National Crime Council of Ireland;2005.

115. Tjaden P. *Full report of the prevalence, indicence, and consequences of violence against women.* Washington, DC: National Institute of Justice;2000.

116. Mihorean K. Trends in self-reported spousal violence. In: Aucoin K, ed. *Family violence in Canada: A statistical profile.* Ottawa: Statistics Canada; 2005.

117. Fantuzzo J. Prevalence of children exposed to domestic violence. Paper presented at: Workshop on Children Exposed to Violence 2002; Washington, DC.

118. Teicher MH, Samson JA, Anderson CM, Ohashi K. The effects of childhood maltreatment on brain structure, function and connectivity. *Nature Reviews Neuroscience.* 2016;17(10):652–66.

119. Gershoff ET. Corporal punishment by parents and associated child behaviors and experiences: A meta-analytic and theoretical review. *Psychological Bulletin.* 2002;128(4):539.

120. Ferguson CJ. Spanking, corporal punishment and negative long-term outcomes: A meta-analytic review of longitudinal studies. *Clinical Psychology Review.* 2013;33(1):196–208.

121. Gershoff ET, Grogan-Kaylor A. Spanking and child outcomes: Old controversies and new meta-analyses. *American Psychological Association*; 2016.

122. Lansford JE, Sharma C, Malone PS, et al. Corporal punishment, maternal warmth, and child adjustment: A longitudinal study in eight countries.

Journal of Clinical Child and Adolescent Psychology.
2014;43(4):670–85.

123. Rebellon CJ, Straus M. Corporal punishment and adult antisocial behavior: A comparison of dyadic concordance types and an evaluation of mediating mechanisms in Asia, Europe, and North America. *International Journal of Behavioral Development.* 2017:0165025417708342.

124. Gershoff ET. Spanking and child development: We know enough now to stop hitting our children. *Child Development Perspectives.* 2013;7(3):133–37.

125. Kitzmann KM, Gaylord NK, Holt AR, Kenny ED. Child witnesses to domestic violence: A meta-analytic review. *Journal of Consulting and Clinical Psychology.* 2003;71(2):339.

126. Chan Y-C, Yeung JW-K. Children living with violence within the family and its sequel: A meta-analysis from 1995–2006. *Aggression and Violent Behavior.* 2009;14(5):313–22.

127. Evans SE, Davies C, DiLillo D. Exposure to domestic violence: A meta-analysis of child and adolescent outcomes. *Aggression and Violent Behavior.* 2008;13(2):131–40.

128. Wolfe D, Crooks C, Lee V, McIntyre-Smith A, Jaffe P. The effects of children's exposure to domestic violence: A meta-analysis and critique. *Clinical Child and Family Psychology Review.* 2003;6(3):171–87.

129. Vu N, Jouriles E, McDonald R, Rosenfield D. Children's exposure to intimate partner violence: A

meta-analysis of longitudinal associations with child adjustment problems. *Clinical Psychology Review.* 2016;45:25–33.

130. Hungerford A, Wait SK, Fritz AM, Clements CM. Exposure to intimate partner violence and children's psychological adjustment, cognitive functioning, and social competence: A review. *Aggression and Violent Behavior.* 2012;17(4):373–82.

131. Howell KH, Barnes SE, Miller LE, Graham-Bermann SA. Developmental variations in the impact of intimate partner violence exposure during childhood. *Journal of Injury and Violence Research.* 2016;8(1):43.

132. Drury SS, Mabile E, Brett ZH, et al. The association of telomere length with family violence and disruption. *Pediatrics.* 2014;134(1):e128–37.

133. Radtke KM, Ruf M, Gunter HM, et al. Transgenerational impact of intimate partner violence on methylation in the promoter of the glucocorticoid receptor. *Translational Psychiatry.* 2011;1(7):e21.

134. Lemmey D, Malecha A, McFarlane J, Willson P, Watson K, et al. Severity of violence against women correlates with behavioral problems in their children. *Pediatric Nursing.* 2001;27(3):265–70.

135. Easterbrooks MA, Katz RC, Kotake C, Stelmach NP, Chaudhuri JH. Intimate partner violence in the first 2 years of life implications for toddlers' behavior regulation. *Journal of Interpersonal Violence.* 2015:0886260515614562.

136. Vu NL, Jouriles EN, McDonald R, Rosenfield D. Children's exposure to intimate partner violence: A meta-analysis of longitudinal associations with child adjustment problems. *Clinical Psychology Review.* 2016;46:25–33.

137. McDonald R, Jouriles E, Tart C, Minze L. Children's adjustment problems in families characterized by men's severe violence toward women: Does other family violence matter? *Child Abuse and Neglect.* 2009;33:94–101.

138. Moore J, Galcius A, Pettican K. Emotional risk to children caught in violent marital conflict: The Basildon treatment project. *Child Abuse and Neglect.* 1981;5:147–52.

139. Holden G, Ritchie K. Linking extreme marital discord, child rearing, and child behavior problems: Evidence from battered women. *Child Development.* 1991;62(2):311–27.

140. Attala J, Summers S. A comparative study of health, developmental, and behavioral factors in preschool children of battered and nonbattered women. *Children's Health Care.* 1999;28(2):189–200.

141. Gleason W. Children of battered women: Developmental delays and behavioral dysfunction. *Violence and Victims.* 1995;10(2):153–60.

142. Graham-Bermann S, Levendosky A. The social functioning of preschool-age children whose mothers are emotionally and physically abused. *Journal of Emotional Abuse.* 1998;1:59–84.

143. Perry B. Incubated in terror: Neurodevelopmental factors in the cycle of violence. In: Osofsky J, ed. *Children, youth, and violence: Searching for solutions.* New York: Guilford Press;1995.

144. Whiteside-Mansell L, Bradley RH, McKelvey L, Fussell JJ. Parenting: Linking impacts of interpartner conflict to preschool children's social behavior. *Journal of Pediatric Nursing.* 10 2009;24(5):389–400.

145. Howell KH, Graham-Bermann SA, Czyz E, Lilly M. Assessing resilience in preschool children exposed to intimate partner violence. *Violence and Victims.* 2010;25(2):150–64.

146. Slopen N, McLaughlin K. Exposure to intimate partner violence and parental depression increases risk of ADHD in preschool children. *Evidence-Based Mental Health.* 2013;16(4):102.

147. Suglia SF, Enlow MB, Kullowatz A, Wright RJ. Maternal intimate partner violence and increased asthma incidence in children: Buffering effects of supportive caregiving. *Archives of Pediatrics and Adolescent Medicine.* 2009;163(3):244–50.

148. Hibel LC, Granger DA, Blair C, Cox MJ, Investigators FLPK. Maternal sensitivity buffers the adrenocortical implications of intimate partner violence exposure during early childhood. *Development and Psychopathology.* 2011;23(2):689.

149. Saltzman K, Holden G, Holahan C. The psychobiology of children exposed to marital violence. *Journal of Clinical Child and Adolescent Psychology.* 2005;34(1):129–39.

150. Kennedy A, Bybee D, Sullivan S, Greeson M. The effects of community and family violence exposure on anxiety trajectories during middle childhood: The role of family social support as a moderator. *Journal of Clinical Child and Adolescent Psychology.* 2009;2009(38):365–79.

151. Iturralde E, Margolin G, Shapiro L. Positive and negative interactions observed between siblings: Moderating effects for children exposed to parents' conflict. *Journal of Research on Adolescence.* 2013;23(4):716–29.

152. Miller LE, VanZomeren-Dohm A, Howell KH, Hunter EC, Graham-Bermann SA. In-home social networks and positive adjustment in children witnessing intimate partner violence. *Journal of Family Issues.* 2014;35(4):462–80.

153. Camacho K, Ehrensaft M, Cohen P. Exposure to intimate partner violence, peer relations, and risk for internalizing behaviors: A prospective longitudinal study. *Journal of Interpersonal Violence.* 2012;27(1):125–41.

154. Graham-Bermann S, Gruber G, Howell K, Girz L. Factors discriminating among profiles of resilience and psychopathology in children exposed to intimate partner violence (IPV). *Child Abuse and Neglect.* 2009;33(9):648–60.

155. Piotrowski CC. Patterns of adjustment among siblings exposed to intimate partner violence. *Journal of Family Psychology.* 2011;25(1):19–28.

156. Agnafors S, Svedin C, Oreland L, Bladh M,

Comasco E, Sydsjo G. A biopsychosocial approach to risk and resilience on behavior in children followed from birth to age 12. *Child Psychiatry and Human Development.* 2016.

157. Fortin A, Doucet M, Damant D. Children's appraisals as mediators of the relationship between domestic violence and child adjustment. *Violence and Victims.* 2011;26(3):377–92.

158. Howell KH, Miller-Graff LE. Protective factors associated with resilient functioning in young adulthood after childhood exposure to violence. *Child Abuse and Neglect.* 2014;38(12):1985–94.

159. Howell KH. Resilience and psychopathology in children exposed to family violence. *Aggression and Violent Behavior.* 2011;16(6):562–69.

160. Ward C, Martin E, Theron C, Distiller G. Factors affecting resilience in children exposed to violence. *South African Journal of Psychology.* 2007;37(1):165–87.

161. Slade A. Parental reflective function: An introduction. *Attachment and Human Development.* 2005;7(3):269–81.

162. Allen J, Fonagy P, Bateman A. Mentalizing. *Mentalizing in Clinical Practice.* Arlington, VA: American Psychiatric Association; 2008:25–72.

163. Steele H, Steele M, Fonagy P. Associations among attachment classifications of mothers, fathers and their infants: Evidence for a relationship-specific perspective. *Child Development.* 1996;76:5411–55.

164. Sharp C, Fonagy P. The parent's capacity to treat the child as a psychological agent: Constructs, measures and implications for developmental psychopathology. *Social Development.* 2008;17(3):737–54.

165. Fonagy P, Gergely G, Jurist E, Target M. *Affect regulation, mentalisation, and the development of the self.* New York: Other Press LLC; 2002.

166. Fonagy P, Steele M, Leigh T, Kennedy RW, Mattoon G, Target M. Attachment, the reflective self and borderline states: The predictive specificity of the Adult Attachment Interview and pathological emotional development. In: S. Goldberg RM, J. Kerr, eds. *Attachment theory: Social, developmental, and clinincal perspectives.* Hillsdale, NJ: Analytic Press; 1995:233–78.

167. Meins E, Fernyhough C. Linguistic acquisition style and mentalizing development: The role of maternal mind-mindedness. *Cognitive Development.* 1999;14:363–80.

168. Meins E, Fernyhough C, Wainwright R, Das Gupta M, Fradley E, Tuckey M. Maternal mind-mindedness and attachment security as predictors of Theory of Mind understanding. *Child Development.* 2002;73(6):1715–26.

169. Laranjo J, Bernier A, Meins E, Carlson S. Early manifestations of children's Theory of Mind: The roles of maternal mind-mindedness and infant security of attachment. *Infancy.* 2010;15(3):300–23.

170. Laranjo J, Bernier A, Meins E, Carlson S. The roles of maternal mind-mindedness and infant security of attachment in predicting preschoolers' understanding of visual perspective taking and false belief. *Journal of Experimental Child Psychology.* 2014;125:48–62.

171. Meins E, Fernyhough C, Wainwright R, et al. Pathways to understanding mind: Construct validity and predictive validity of maternal mind-mindedness. *Child Development.* 2003;74(4):1194–1211.

172. Meins E, Fernyhough C, de Rosnay M, Arnott B, Leekam SR, Turner M. Mind-mindedness as a multidimensional construct: Appropriate and nonattuned mind-related comments independently predict infant–mother attachment in a socially diverse sample. *Infancy.* 2012;17(4):393–415.

173. National Scientific Council on the Developing Child. *Establishing a level foundation for life: Mental health begins in early childhood.* Boston, MA: Center on the Developing Child at Harvard University;2008/2012.

174. Marmot M, Friel S, Bell R, Houweling T, Taylor T, Commission on Social Determinants of Health. Closing the gap in a generation: Healthy equity through action on the social determinants of health. *Lancet.* 2008;372:1661–69.

175. Stewart M. *Integrating social support in nursing.* New York, NY: Sage;1993.

176. Gottlieb B. *Social support strategies: Guidelines for mental health practice.* Vol 7. Beverly Hills, CA: Sage;1983.

177. Zemp M, Milek A, Cummings EM, Cina A, Bodenmann G. How couple- and parenting-focused programs affect child behavioral problems: A randomized controlled trial. *Journal of Child and Family Studies.* 2016;25(3):798–810.

178. Braithwaite DO, McBride MC, Schrodt P. "Parent teams" and the everyday interactions of co-parenting in stepfamilies. *Communication Reports.* 2003;16(2):93–111.

179. Pruett M, Cowan C, Cowan P, Pruett K. Lessons learned from the Supporting Father Involvement Study: A cross-cultural preventive intervention for low-income families with young children. *Journal of Social Services Research.* 2009;35(2):163–79.

180. Short E, Riggs DW, Perlesz A, Brown R, Kane G. Lesbian, gay, bisexual and transgender (LGBT) parented families. *Melbourne: The Australian Psychological Society.* 2007.

181. Conger RD, Schofield TJ, Neppl TK, Merrick MT. Disrupting intergenerational continuity in harsh and abusive parenting: The importance of a nurturing relationship with a romantic partner. *Journal of Adolescent Health.* 2013;53(4):S11–17.

182. Cohen S, Underwood L, Gottlieb B, eds. *Social support measurement and intervention: A guide for health and social scientists.* New York: Oxford University Press; 2002.

183. Lin N, Ye X, Ensel WM. Social support and depressed mood: A structural analysis. *J Health Soc Behav.* Dec 1999;40(4):344–59.

184. Dennis CL. Peer support within a health care context: A concept analysis. *International Journal of Nursing Studies.* Mar 2003;40(3):321–32.

185. Hanna BA, Edgecombe G, Jackson CA, Newman S. The importance of first-time parent groups for new parents. *Nursing and Health Sciences.* 2002;4(4):209–14.

A more detailed reference list is available from the author on request.

Credits

Chapter 1

31–33   Reproduced by permission from V.J. Felitti et al., "Relationship of childhood abuse and household dysfunction to many of the leading causes of death in adults: The Adverse Childhood Experiences (ACE) study." *American Journal of Preventive Medicine* 14, no. 4 (1998): 245–58.

Chapter 2

51   Adapted from Human Resources Development Canada and Statistics Canada National Longitudinal Survey of Children and Youth, User's Handbook and Microdata Guide, cycle 1, release 2 (public domain). Minister of Industry,

Ottawa (1997). Available at www.statcan.ca /english/freepub/89F0078XIE/free.htm

Also adapted from
S.R. Doyle & C.A. McCarty (2000). Parent Questionnaire (Grade 4+), Grade 5 Update (Technical Report Addendum). Available at https://fasttrackproject.org/techrept/p/prq/ prq6add.pdf

Chapter 4

86–87   Adapted from public domain measure printed in L.S. Radloff, "The CES-D scale: A self-report depression scale for research in the general population. *Applied Psychological Measurement* 1, (1977): 385–401.

Chapter 5

107–109   Adapted from reference in the public domain. A. Pokorny, B. Miller, H. Kaplan, "The brief MAST: A shortened version of the Michigan Alcoholism Screening Test." *American Journal of Psychiatry* 129, no. 3 (1972): 342–5.

Chapter 8

168–70   Used with permission from G. Zimet, N. Dahlem, S. Zimet, & G. Farley, "The multidimensional scale of perceived social support." *The Journal of Personality Assessment* 52, no. 1 (1988) 30–41; and G. Zimet,

S. Powell, G. Farley, S. Werkman, & K. Berkoff, "Psychometric characteristics of the MSPSS." *Journal of Personality Assessment* 55, no. 3–4 (1990): 610–17; and I. Clara, B. Cox, M. Enns, L. Murray, & L. Torgrudc, "Confirmatory factor analysis of the MSPSS in clinically distressed and student samples." *Journal of Personality Assessment* 81, no. 3 (2003): 265–70.

BOOK CREDITS

Acquiring Editor: Carrie Gleason
Editor: Elena Radic
Proofreader: Jennifer Dinsmore

Designer: Laura Boyle
E-Book Designer: Carmen Giraudy

Publicist: Michelle Melski

DUNDURN

Publisher: Kirk Howard
Acquisitions: Scott Fraser
Managing Editor: Kathryn Lane
Director of Design and Production: Jennifer Gallinger
Marketing Manager: Kate Condon-Moriarty
Sales Manager: Synora Van Drine

Editorial: Allison Hirst, Dominic Farrell, Jenny McWha, Rachel Spence, Elena Radic
Design and Production: Laura Boyle, Carmen Giraudy, Lorena Gonzalez Guillen
Marketing and Publicity: André Bovee-Begun, Michelle Melski, Kendra Martin

dundurn.com   dundurnpress
@dundurnpress   dundurnpress
dundurnpress   info@dundurn.com

FIND US ON NETGALLEY & GOODREADS TOO!

DUNDURN